# THE SKY IS NOT FALLING

## LIVING FEARLESSLY IN THESE TURBULENT TIMES

# CHARLES COLSON

*NEW YORK TIMES* BEST-SELLING AUTHOR

## WORTHY
PUBLISHING

Published by Worthy Publishing, a division of Worthy Media, Inc., 134 Franklin Road, Suite 200, Brentwood, Tennessee 37027.

HELPING PEOPLE EXPERIENCE THE HEART OF GOD

ISBN 978-1-61793-134-5

Cover Design: Christopher Tobias, Tobias Design
Umbrella Image: © pixhook/iStockphoto.com
Interior Design and Typesetting: Inside Out Design and Typesetting

*Printed in the United States of America*

# CONTENTS

# Publisher's Note

Charles Colson is widely respected as a keen observer of matters of faith and culture, and a leading voice on the issues that have shaped our society. Over the years, he has imparted his wisdom and poignant insights in the pages of *Christianity Today*. Many of those ideas are woven together here, offering enduring hope and fresh perspective for our times.

# FOREWORD

When some future historian 100 years from now writes the history of American evangelicalism, the life and work of Chuck Colson will have a large role in the story. His own life story is compelling.

Born in Boston when Herbert Hoover was president of the United States, Colson graduated from Brown University, served his country in the United States Marines, became an accomplished lawyer, and eventually served as Special Counsel to President Richard M. Nixon. Caught up in the scandal of Watergate, Colson fell from the pinnacle of power and soon found himself serving time in an Alabama jail. Out of this shattering experience, he was converted to Jesus Christ, an experience he wrote about in his best-selling book, *Born Again* (1976). While still in prison, God gave Chuck Colson a vision for a ministry to prisoners and their families. Out of his vision came Prison Fellowship, the world's largest prison outreach program, which is now chartered in 120 countries around the world.

In the early days of Prison Fellowship, many people thought that Colson was just another flash in the pan. Sadly, the evangelical world has far too many Elmer Gantry-type celebrities who use their fame to promote and enrich themselves at the expense of others. Would Colson be another one of these? Many people wondered. Would he have staying power?

Now, more than three and a half decades later, even Colson's sternest critics have to admit that he is the "real thing."

Eugene Peterson once described the life of faith as "a long obedience in the same direction." This is the story of Colson's career as a prison reformer, columnist, author, and respected statesman in the world Christian movement. Here is a man of God who shows his faith by his works. Since the late seventies, Colson has visited more than 600 prisons in forty countries. With the help of tens of thousands of volunteers, he has developed effective programs in restorative justice, community care, inner-city renewal, rehabilitation, and a network of loving support for the children of prisoners, appropriately named Angel Tree. Colson knows by experience the life-transforming power of Jesus Christ and he expends himself sharing this with others—the least, the last, the lost. In recognition of his work, Colson received the prestigious million-dollar Templeton Prize for Progress in Religion in 1993, which he donated to Prison Fellowship, as he does all his speaking fees and book royalties.

In recent years, Colson has come to see more clearly the connection between genuine prison reform and the wider social and ethical issues that influence our culture today. At a time when some voices are suggesting that the church should just "stick with its knitting" and avoid taking a stand on any issue at stake in the public square, Colson has emerged as a major voice calling on Christian believers everywhere to recognize the lordship of Jesus Christ upon our whole life. This is not a call for Christians to be more "political" in the sense of embracing the agenda of any partisan movement or ideology. Colson's approach is, rather, a summons to first principles—a recognition that there are moral absolutes we can violate only at our peril, that utopian solutions to social problems are vacuous and counterproductive, that the rule of law has a respected place in the ordering of a just society but that Christians have a non-negotiable commitment to "render unto Caesar that which is Caesar's, but under no circumstances to render unto Caesar that which is God's."

That last sentence is from the closing lines of the Manhattan Declaration, a statement of Christian conscience drafted by Chuck Colson, Robert George, and me, and signed by more than 500,000 Catholic, Orthodox, and Evangelical believers. It affirms the sanctity of human life from conception to natural death, the dignity of marriage as a lifelong covenantal union between one man and one woman, and religious freedom for all persons everywhere. The Manhattan Declaration is closely related to another initiative Colson has developed, a six-part video series titled *Doing the Right Thing*. This is an effort to move beyond a program of ethics based on keeping rules and complying with government regulations. *Doing the Right Thing* asks fundamental questions about the underlying assumptions that undergird our public acts. It calls for a renewal of duty, integrity, fidelity, humility, and the kind of spirituality that recognizes life itself as a gift from God.

For the past two decades, I have had the privilege of knowing Chuck Colson and working closely with him in many endeavors including Evangelicals and Catholics Together, a movement for Christian unity founded by Colson and the late Father Richard John Neuhaus. I have been with Colson when he has visited prisons and preached the gospel to men and women behind bars. I have sat with him through difficult board meetings and have shared his struggles over how to do the right thing in the right way. I have seen him embrace little children and reach out to brothers and sisters on the margins of society. In these and many other situations, I have seen the love of Christ shine through.

Chuck Colson has a prophetic word for today's church. He shares it here with conviction, compassion, and rare wisdom.

—TIMOTHY GEORGE
Chairman of the Board, *BreakPoint*;
Founding Dean, Beeson Divinity School, Samford University

# INTRODUCTION

The 2008 elections left moral conservatives perplexed, and no wonder.[1] Even though 70 percent of Americans oppose partial-birth abortion, voters placed in office a president and congressional majorities in both houses that favor it. Even though the majority of Americans strongly oppose so-called same-sex "marriage," voters elected both a congress and an administration that strongly support it. Though the majority of Americans hold views to the right of center, voters elected a government that is more left of center than any in our nation's history.

The results deepen a malaise I've sensed among evangelicals over our ability to change the culture. On all sides I hear battle-weary Christians talk about abandoning cultural engagement and tending our own backyard instead.

Like other leaders in Christian ministries, I know the most effective fundraising is to screech that the sky is falling, but we should resist that temptation. We should inspire hope.

The most compelling reason for hope comes from looking beyond any current election at deeper, long-term historical trends. The twentieth century was the age of ideology, of the great "isms": communism, socialism, nazism, liberalism, humanism, scientism. Everywhere, ideologues nursed visions of creating the ideal society by some utopian scheme. Whether by revolution or racial purity or scientific technology, these True Believers set out to build a modern Tower of Babel, reaching to the heavens (metaphorically, since most were aggressively secular).

The attitude was captured in the film *Titanic*, when a passenger glances proudly at the ship and declares, "Even God himself could not sink it."

Other idols have sunk just as surely, if not as quickly. Nazism was forever disgraced by the horrors of its concentration camps. The Soviet Union crumbled with the Berlin Wall. Around the globe formerly socialist nations have eagerly lined up to establish free economies. Liberalism, while still powerful, has lost its luster: American politicians eschew the label. Even science often seems a Frankenstein's monster turning on its creators.

This was the most significant fact at the end of the twentieth century: all the major ideological constructions had failed, tossed on the ash heap of history. For all were based on the same underlying theme: liberate the individual from the oppression of family, church, and local custom, and he would be autonomous and free. But today it is clear that weakening the moral bonds of family, church, and neighborhood does not lead to freedom but to alienation, loneliness, disorder, and crime—and even to the rise of the totalitarian state.

The dream of autonomy has turned into a nightmare of chaos and coercion. Today the tide is turning as Americans grow desperate for the security found in the moral bonds of family and community.

The only remaining "ism" is postmodernism, which is not an ideology but a repudiation of all ideologies. Its relativism is the admission that every attempt to construct a comprehensive, utopian worldview has failed. It is a formalized expression of despair.

Only one compelling claim to transcendent truth remains, one secure hope: Christianity. The church has stood unshaken through the ebb and flow of two millennia. It has survived both the barbarian invasions of the Middle Ages and the intellectual assaults of the modern era. Its solid walls rise up above the ruins littered across the intellectual landscape.

This moment, when the culture at large is facing the bankruptcy of its systems, is the worst possible time for Christians to despair. On the contrary, it is time for us to blow trumpets and fly the flag high. To desert the field of battle now would be historical blindness, betraying our heritage just when we have the greatest opportunity we may ever face. This is the time to make a compelling case that Christianity offers the only rational and realistic hope for both personal redemption and social renewal.

This is not a Pollyanna vision of our culture which ignores the depth of our cultural, governmental, economic, and ethical problems or pretends they are not real and serious. They are appallingly real and deadly serious. And if they are not checked, the sky will fall. Our culture will collapse as surely as that of ancient Israel when they turned away from the protective and life-sustaining principles of God. But collapse is far from inevitable because the church has in its purpose, worldview, ethos, and mission everything needed to turn culture around.

This book, woven, adapted, and updated from articles I've written in *Christianity Today* over the past dozen years, addresses many of the problems visibly apparent in culture today and shows how the church has the answer that can yet save us, if we apply it. Never has it been more important for Christians to remain engaged in the task of cultural renewal—to stay at our posts. And if we are steadfast, we have no reason to fear that shards of the wild blue yonder will come crashing down on our heads.

# 1

# CLIMBING THE GREAT IDEOLOGICAL DIVIDE

# 1

## CLIMBING THE GREAT
## IDEOLOGICAL DIVIDE

Among sophisticates on Manhattan's Upper East Side and in Georgetown salons, President Bush's election in November of 2000 brought much wailing, gnashing of teeth, and rending of (fashionable) garments.[1] Disgruntled "blue" voters threatened to move overseas to escape the "jihadists" and "mullahs" now running—and ruining—America.

Four years later, in a column entitled "Two Nations Under God," the *New York Times*'s Thomas Friedman said he woke up the morning after Bush's reelection "deeply troubled" because "they [Bush and company] favor a whole different kind of America from me." Amen, echoed Tina Brown in the *Washington Post*: "New Yorkers don't want to live in a republic of fear."

But then the November elections of 2008 left moral conservatives perplexed as well, and no wonder. With the victories of Barak Obama and resounding Democratic majorities in both the House and Senate, it seemed to them that the nation had been taken over by something close to a hostile power.

As these laments from both sides of the spectrum demonstrate, what we witnessed in these elections is a continuing deepening of hostilities between "red" and "blue" states—"Retros" and "Metros." Historian Gertrude Himmelfarb described this phenomenon as two cultures existing within one nation. She believes these two can coexist peacefully; I wonder. Americans are engaged in a civil war carried on by other means; as with the first Civil War, fundamental issues divide us.

## A CULTURAL GRAND CANYON

How did we get into this mess? Some suggest it started when secular forces pressed their views on abortion and gay rights in court. In part, that's so. But I think we must look deeper. We dug the hole that became a cultural Grand Canyon when we abandoned belief in a moral truth that is knowable.

People who reject transcendent authority can no longer persuade one another through rational arguments; everything is reduced to personal opinion. Debates about ideas thus degenerate into power struggles; we're left with no moral standard by which to measure the common good. For that matter, how can there be a "common good" without an objective standard of truth?

The death of moral truth has fractured America into two warring camps, with each side's preferences hardening into an ideology. And ideology is the enemy of revealed truth. It's also the enemy of classical conservatism, which depends, as Russell Kirk wrote, upon tradition and the accumulated wisdom of the past; ideology, on the other hand, is a human scheme for how the world ought to be formed. Whether on the Left or the Right, ideologies are utopian—the dangerous idea that we can construct the perfect society.

This is why politics has become so ugly today. When I first worked on Capitol Hill in the 1950s, there was camaraderie among politicians. Democrats dropped into our office to chat with us. People on both sides of the aisle met in the local lounge for drinks after work. Of course, we had disagreements. But when it came to questions like how we were going to take care of the poor, our differences were over degree and means. Everybody shared common ideas about what made a good society.

Not anymore. Today, ideologies are irreconcilable. Along with lower taxes, religious conservatives argue for moral order, respect for tradition, protection of life and religious expression. Many secularists, by contrast, dismiss the idea that the government should enforce any moral good. Indeed, they want government to protect individuals from having any such standards imposed on them: radical libertarianism.

This is at the heart of the culture war—why the "reds" and "blues" are locked in mortal combat. It's a struggle for ultimate power. Ultimate power is what moves in to fill the vacuum when a society loses its consensus on the validity of moral absolutes as the basis for a common worldview. And I can attest from personal experience that we are losing—or more disturbingly, have already lost—our communal sense of moral absolutes.

## What's Wrong with This Picture?

Over the years, I've often taught worldview to groups of bright young students. With each group, I had the same distressing experience. When I presented a classic example of a self-refuting moral proposition, they just didn't get it.

An example: the late Christopher Reeve, in his wheelchair with a breathing tube, was testifying before a Senate committee. Reeve dismissed moral objections to embryonic stem-cell research, claiming that the purpose of government is "to serve the greatest good for the greatest number."

I then asked the students, "What's wrong with this picture?" When I got no answers I dropped heavy hints. Only one student gave the correct answer: if what Reeve advocated actually were our governing philosophy, he would not have been there to testify. Who would spend millions to keep him alive when that money could help thousands?

I don't know whether the students lacked analytical skills or were just confused, but when I explained the inherent contradiction, the lights finally went on. When I discussed the concept of absolute truth, and the fact that it is knowable, there was an occasional nod of understanding, but it was clear I was breaking new ground. These students, mind you, were products of Christian homes and schools.

This lack of worldview awareness is appalling—but it's exactly what the Barna Group found in a recent poll: just 9 percent of evangelical students believe in anything called absolute truth. What does this say about the job our schools, our families, and our churches are doing?

## POST POSTMODERNISM

Let's tackle the schools first. Many Christians—like former Prison Fellowship president Mark Earley, who spent thirteen years in public office—support the public school system. They believe Christian students ought to be part of it and provide a Christian influence. Mark has practiced what he preaches, sending his six children to public schools.

But for the first time in his life, Mark is having real doubts. The problem is that diversity training—in which students are told it's wrong to make truth claims of any kind—has been impressed in the minds of our children. This twisted interpretation of tolerance makes it an offense even to make truth claims—or judge the ideas and behaviors of others.

This abhorrence of any claim to absolute truth comes from the postmodern mindset, which asserts that we can have no "grand metanarrative" that makes sense of reality. Since there's no such thing as truth, all principles are merely personal preferences. The growing prevalence of that mindset does much to explain why we are presently engaged in a new civil war. As professor Ed Veith explains, the postmodernist claims that all you can do is try to impose your preferences on others before they impose theirs on you.

We can see why postmodernism leads to warlike rancor when we examine its roots. As a philosophy, postmodernism draws inspiration from the writings of nineteenth-century philosopher Friedrich Nietzsche, who argued that "languages of good and evil" are rooted in neither truth nor reason, but in the will to power. In the 1930s the Nazis fleshed out Nietzsche's ideas, resulting in horrific consequences.

While the Western powers defeated the Nazis, we did not defeat the philosophy that incited them. In the *Atlantic Monthly*, political scientist Francis Fukuyama says the decline in traditional morality in the West can be traced most directly to

Nietzsche's view that moral principles are not objective; they are cultural inventions that serve as smokescreens for power struggles. And since they are "socially constructed," they must be "deconstructed" to unmask the underlying power grab.

Thus, subverting authority becomes a good thing, breaking the rules an act of liberation. This explains why the word *transgression* from the King James Version of the Bible has become a shibboleth in some academic circles. As literary critic Roger Shattuck writes, postmodernists have "transform[ed] sin and evil into a positive term: 'transgression.'" They praise "transgressive" acts for breaking down oppressive moral rules.

## NIETZSCHE'S LEGACY

The late Michel Foucault even praised irrational violence as a way to be liberated from rules imposed in the name of reason. As these ideas filter down to popular culture, movies and rap music depict murderers as confident, efficient, unflappable. Cool. And eventually kids, like the two Nazi-imitating teenagers at Columbine High School near Littleton, Colorado, in 1999, shoot down their classmates while laughing.

A historical parallel to Littleton took place eighty-five years ago when two college students, Nathan Leopold and Richard Loeb, murdered a fourteen-year-old boy. Their defense lawyer was the infamous Clarence Darrow, and his most dramatic appeal was to argue that Leopold had absorbed the ideas of Nietzsche at school. "Your Honor," he said, "it is hardly fair to hang a nineteen-year-old boy for the philosophy that was taught him at the university."

In both cases, of course, the murderers were accountable for their actions. Yet the Littleton killers were acting out the logical consequences of a postmodernism taught today from university to grade school. They were mirroring in grotesque action what the adult culture advocates in abstract concepts.

Francis Schaeffer taught a method of pre-evangelism that presses people to the logical consequences of their own beliefs. Littleton, as well as Leopold and Loeb, illustrate what Nietzsche's philosophy leads to when lived out in the real world. It is one thing to debate the topic in a rarefied academic setting; it's quite another when a Nazi-quoting teenager sticks a gun in your face. Suddenly, you realize that worldviews do matter.

Littleton also brought into bold relief the contrast between Nietzsche's legacy and the Christian worldview. The killers harbored a fierce hatred of Christianity and reportedly asked some victims if they believed in God before killing them. Included among the martyred teens were Rachel Scott, the first to be killed, who was told to "go be with him" and was shot in the head when she answered "yes"; Cassie Bernall, who was later found with her hands still clasped in prayer; and Valeen Schnurr, who survived multiple gunshot wounds after she also answered "yes."

Who can forget the news photos of crosses on the hill for the slain? Or the interviews with Christian parents offering forgiveness and reconciliation? Or the funeral services broadcasting the gospel message across the nation? I cannot remember any event in recent years that produced such stunning Christian testimony.

God is not mocked. A vicious attack on his people was turned into a powerful demonstration of faith overcoming evil. These teens inspired others. Across the country, youth pastors reported revivals. At Cassie Bernall's church alone, attendance increased by 500 people. *Time* magazine even ran a two-page spread on the stunning revival among teens.

## Competing Worldviews

Littleton brought us face to face with the two sides of today's civil war—the two worldviews competing for our allegiance—a postmodernism rooted in the will to power, contrasted with a biblical faith rooted in the will of God. Which will America choose? There is considerable evidence to suggest that many are now ready to make the right choice.

If you hold your ear close to the ground in Washington, D.C., the rumble you will hear is not the Metro but a populist rage hurtling like a railroad train toward the Capitol. Americans have by and large lost faith in their institutions, and the evidence is everywhere. According to a CBS News poll, at the beginning of the new millennium, 45 percent of Americans trusted government to do the right thing most of the time. Now less than 25 percent do so. A January 2010 joint poll by NBC and the *Wall Street Journal* found that the percentage of people who view the president negatively had nearly doubled in a year's time. Approval ratings for Congress were even lower: 21 percent, and had subsequently dropped into the single digits by 2011, according to a Rasmussen poll.

In some respects, the distrust is justified. Hurricane Katrina was a blow that the Bush Administration never fully recovered from, just as ineffective response to the 2010 Gulf Oil Spill did untold damage to the Obama Administration. A cumbersome government bureaucracy too slow in providing help shattered citizens' faith in government's effectiveness.

But the ineffectiveness of government was magnified in the case of the Nigerian terrorist who almost brought down a Northwest airliner headed for Detroit in December 2009. Brave passengers, not a massive government apparatus, thwarted him. In the postmortem, we discovered that despite a multitrillion-dollar campaign to protect citizens against terrorism, and the fact that the visa office in Lagos, Nigeria, had been warned that Umar Farouq Abdulmutallab was dangerous, it issued him a visa anyway. Appalling.

The bigger that government gets, the further it grows from the people. From the massive expansion of health care to increased environmental controls, higher taxes, and mind-numbing budget deficits, people feel overwhelmed and powerless. It doesn't help when Congress closes its doors to draw up the health-care bill in conference committee—signaling a request to the public not to butt into its affairs.

Where will all of this lead? There are a few likely scenarios. Government could get a dose of reality and put the brakes on. But its leaders give us no indication of restraining themselves. A second scenario could drive us off a cliff into national bankruptcy, which has happened in many countries whose governments spend irresponsibly. The third possibility, and the one I think we are on the verge of witnessing, is that the civil war over which philosophy will dominate how we are governed could spur a populist revolt.

Populist movements in the U.S. can be healthy, as when Andrew Jackson broke the grip of the Eastern elite on the presidency, or when William Jennings Bryan, three-time Democratic candidate for president, led a movement to give greater voice to the disillusioned masses. But this time, a massive wave of anti-government sentiment could shatter the political consensus, which may well leave the country virtually unmanageable.

## Red, Blue and Black and White

The inevitable consequence of all of this should deeply trouble Christians, who, of any segment of our society, understand the necessity of a strong government. The Bible teaches that God ordains government, appoints leaders, and requires obedience so that we might live peaceable lives.

Why is this? God recognizes that among fallen humans in a fallen world, even a bad government is better than no government. No government leads to chaos and mob rule. When order breaks down, justice is inevitably undermined. As Augustine of Hippo argued, peace flows from order, and both are necessary preconditions to the preservation of liberty and some measure of human dignity and flourishing.

This is why great leaders of the faith throughout history have held government in such high esteem. Some, such as John Calvin, considered the magistrate the highest of vocations.

Of course, while we have a high view of government, it isn't a blank check. Christian doctrines such as sphere sovereignty, subsidiarity (nothing should be done by a larger, complex organization when a smaller organization can accomplish it), the balance of power, and God's transcendent law must hold government in check. So if Washington has lost touch with the people, as

Christians we should work fervently to reform these systems. Real reform may even have to come through an independent commission like Securing America's Future Economy (SAFE), for which Congressman Frank Wolf has tirelessly advocated.

The tea party movement may have a lot of traction in America today, but it makes no attempt to present a governing philosophy. It simply seeks an outlet—an understandable one—for the brooding frustrations of many Americans. But anti-government attitudes are not the substitute for good government. We should be instructing people enraged at the excesses of Washington and the growing ethical malaise in the Capitol to focus their rage at fixing government, not throwing the baby out with the bath water.

We Christians are to be the best citizens, praying for our leaders and holding them in high regard, even as we push for the reforms desperately needed to keep representative government flourishing. Only when we funnel frustrations into constructive reformation can we expect a government that is truly of the people, by the people, and for the people.

Until we have such a government, we will continue to witness today's civil war as the two factions fight for control. This is why we're seeing such hysterical rhetoric from the Left, which, with the loss of the House in 2010, fears it's losing its power—and power is all that matters. The Right is just as bad. Some leaders now say that the Republicans will try to impose their will on everyone else—an attitude repugnant to democratic governance.

What's the solution?

First, "red" Christians must reach out to "blue" Christians and vice versa. Ideology must not divide believers. Second,

Christians are not seeking political power, so we're not out to "destroy" perceived political enemies. Nor do we line up for the victor's spoils, as if we were just one more special-interest group. Instead, we need to graciously contend (and demonstrate) that Christian truth is good for the right ordering of our lives, individually and collectively, and manifest our commitment to the common good by doing the things Christians do best: creating strong families, restoring relationships, helping the poor, working for human rights.

Christians are in a unique position to bring common grace to a deeply divided nation and offer something more than brief periods of peace between outbreaks of mortal combat every election cycle. In rejecting ideology and putting the common good first, we offer hope to America's warring factions.

# 2

# CONFRONTING
# POSTMODERNISM

# CONFRONTING

# POSTMODERNISM

In the late 1990s, there was a growing clamor to throw David Cash, a student at the University of California at Berkeley, out of the school.[1] The controversy over Cash arose from a gruesome case a year earlier in which a California teenager, Jeremy Strohmeyer, sexually molested and murdered a seven-year-old girl in a Las Vegas casino. Cash witnessed what his friend was doing but did not stop him and later agreed to keep quiet. Strohmeyer pled guilty to sexual assault and murder. But failing to prevent a crime is not itself a crime, so Cash blithely finished high school and went on to Berkeley.

Afterward he remained defiantly unrepentant. "Were you appalled that a friend said he had killed a little girl?" the *Los Angeles Times* asked him. Cash answered: "I'm not going to get upset over someone else's life. I just worry about myself first."

This murder is one more bone-chilling example of teens and college students slaying in cold blood, without remorse or conscience. Over recent years, several children have walked into schoolyards across the country and fired on their classmates—in Arkansas, Oregon, Kentucky, Mississippi, Pennsylvania, and Minnesota. In fact, since the 1999 massacre at Columbine, there have been sixty shootings in schools and colleges, resulting in 106 deaths. Most of the perpetrators were in their teens or twenties. The news media and pundits have cast about for explanations. When such crimes occur, the government consistently announces that we need stricter gun controls; but in almost every case, the guns were registered. Other explanations offered for crime are poverty or race, but almost all of these kids were middle class and white.

What is frightening is precisely how normal most of them seem. In New Jersey, Amy Grossburg and her boyfriend checked into a hotel room, gave birth, and killed the baby. Another teen, the "Prom Mom," gave birth in a restroom, dumped the baby in the trash, and returned to finish the dance. These were ordinary teens—except that they murdered their babies, violating the most primal human instinct.

Reporters have raised all the conventional explanations except one. They could not bring themselves to use the dreaded "m-word": *morality*. The truth is that Americans are losing their moral recognition of the universal dignity of human life. Like Cash, they dehumanize their victims. In the sentencing of Grossburg, the judge said he was troubled by "an egocentricity that blinded you to . . . the intrinsic value of the life of the child."

Where are the adults who are supposed to teach these kids the intrinsic value of human life and other moral absolutes? Adults who once gave firm moral direction—parents, pastors, teachers—too often buy the myth that they should refrain from teaching kids right from wrong, and rather let them discover their own values. Other adults are busy producing and selling entertainment that glorifies violence, teaching kids exactly the wrong things. Strohmeyer told police he strangled the little girl by twisting her neck the way he had seen in movies. And it's a no-brainer that young people today imitate the sexual mores they see in movies, on the TV screen, and in Internet videos. We are raising a generation of children conditioned to scrap all moral absolutes.

It's enough to make one despair of American civilization itself. But as Christians, we should resist that temptation and instead turn social breakdown into an opportunity to make a compelling case for biblical morality. One strategy for evangelism, Francis Schaeffer taught, is to press people to the logical conclusions of their basic presuppositions: to show people that their assumptions, if lived out consistently, would lead to destructive and inhumane consequences. Today people are beginning to recognize the soul-destroying consequences of postmodernism, and now is the time to press them to see the wisdom of biblical truth.

When kids kill kids, people can no longer tolerate the chaos created by moral autonomy. The bill on postmodernism is coming due. Either we will pay its bloody price or find our way back to the truths that make civilization possible.

## The Roots of Moral Chaos

The disregard for absolute morality we are witnessing today does not happen without cause. A number of societal influences have contributed to our drift away from the strong sense of truth that once characterized this nation. Not the least of these is the value-free nature of our current educational system from the primary grades through the university.

When David Cash returned to school after passively witnessing Strohmeyer's brutal act, seventy-five outraged citizens gathered outside Cash's dormitory with bullhorns, shouting, "Expel him!"

What most people overlook, however, is that Cash's attitude accords precisely with the postmodernist philosophy propagated by places like Berkeley. The core of postmodernism is a rejection of universal truth claims and moral principles. And if there are no universal ideals linking us together, then logically all that's left are "tribes": identity groups based on race, ethnicity, gender, sexual orientation, or whatever. On a radio talk show, Cash said of the murder, "It's a tragic event, okay. But the simple fact remains that I do not know this girl. The only person I knew in this event was Jeremy Strohmeyer." In other words, the victim was not a member of his "tribe," his identity group. Strohmeyer was. His only obligation, he concluded, was to his buddy.

This tribal orientation is why virtually every state university today has separate dorms for students who are black, Asian, Hispanic, homosexual, or any other group demanding a separate identity. No one is permitted to judge another group's actions or beliefs, because there is no recognition of ultimate truths binding on everyone. These ideas percolate down from academia to shape our moral attitudes.

Expel Cash from Berkeley? No: make him its poster boy. Cash's moral indifference is the inevitable result of today's trendy campus ideology; his actions are postmodernist logic carried to its grotesque conclusion.

A few years ago I spoke at my alma mater, Brown University, arguing that without acknowledging moral truth, it's impossible for colleges to teach ethics. I've been saying this since the late 1980s, all over America, and I've yet to be successfully contradicted. Whenever someone claims *his* alma mater teaches ethics, I ask him to send me the curriculum, which invariably turns out to be pure pragmatism, utilitarianism, or social issues like diversity and the environment—good things, but not ethics.

Ethics—in fact, any claim of absolute truth or morality—is anathema in contemporary universities, and that mindset has trickled down even to the primary grades of public schools. How can we expect our children to behave morally and hold to a high standard of truth when those ideals are sliced from them in our schools? As C.S. Lewis said, "We laugh at honor and are shocked to find traitors in our midst. We castrate and bid the geldings be fruitful."[2]

## BLAMING IT ON THE "SELFISH GENE"

Another destructive influence on our sense of absolutes is the prevalence of Darwinian evolution in our basic assumptions. Richard Dawkins, the flamboyant British biologist who gave us the phrase "selfish genes," now offers a genetic explanation for the sexual foibles of our nation's leaders, such as Presidents John F. Kennedy and Bill Clinton, vice presidential candidate John Edwards, former South Carolina governor Mark Sanford, and the late Senator Ted Kennedy. Our evolutionary ancestors were harem builders (like seals), Dawkins explains, instead of being monogamous (like Canadian geese). Any male monopolizing power and wealth also monopolized the females, thus ensuring the survival of his genes. The behavior of so many of our leaders is simply a fossilized remnant from our genetic past.

Well, Dawkins's Just-So story may be good for a chuckle. But reducing human behavior to genetics is serious business these days. The latest fad is an updated version of sociobiology known as evolutionary psychology, which seeks explanations for human behavior in our genes. Evolutionary psychology is popular because it promises to fill a gap in the Darwinist worldview: the need for a workable morality. Ever since Darwin, many have recognized that evolution leads to moral nihilism. Evolutionary psychology claims that by examining our evolutionary history, we can identify which behaviors have been selected for their adaptive value. These provide the basis for a genuinely scientific morality.

Does this new theory succeed in rescuing evolution from moral nihilism? No. The first problem is that any behavior practiced anywhere can be judged to have survival value—after all, it has *survived*—including behavior widely considered immoral.

In an article in the *New York Times*, Steven Pinker, a telegenic science popularizer, urges us to "understand" teenage girls who kill their newborns, arguing that "the emotional circuitry of mothers has evolved" by natural selection to include "a capacity for neonaticide." Infanticide is built into our "biological design," and we can't blame people for doing it.

The big clash of evolutionary psychology with absolute values is found in its genetic determinism. It claims to base morality on the genes that govern our behavior, leaving us free from moral responsibility for our choices and actions. If genes really do that, moral choice is an illusion. In *The Moral Animal,* Robert Wright spends hundreds of pages denouncing freedom as an illusion and describing human beings as "robots," "machines," and "puppets" of our genes. Then he turns 180 degrees, arguing that we are free to choose moral ideals contrary to the "values" of natural selection.

Fatal contradictions such as this make hash of every effort to derive morality from biology—and Christians need to press the point in our classrooms and living rooms. Yet in spite of these contradictions, evolutionary psychology is being dished up to an anxious public via magazine and newspaper articles. In an era dogged by declining morality and social decay, it offers the soothing promise of a morality buttressed by the certitude of science—as well as an escape from moral responsibility.

Make no mistake. The goal of evolutionary psychology is utterly radical: to replace traditional religious morality with a new scientific morality. The strategy is to debunk traditional morality by reducing it to genetic self-interest. Wright is typical: he unmasks all "thoughts and feelings," all "moral values," as "stratagems of the genes." Even Jesus' teachings are nothing but ideologies serving his "evolutionarily ingrained interests." Evolutionary psychology proposes to base morality frankly on "selfish genes."

Some Christians have hoped to make peace with Darwinism as long as it is restricted to biology. But evolutionary psychology demonstrates that there is an inexpungible imperialism in Darwinianism—a compulsion to reduce all society to material mechanisms. Just as Darwinist theory in biology aims to replace divine design with natural processes, so in ethics it aims to replace revealed morality with a naturalistic morality. Sociologist

Howard Kaye observes evolutionary psychology is nothing less than a secularized natural theology—an attempt to use nature to justify a secular worldview freed from moral absolutes.

In his 1898 Princeton lectures, Dutch statesman Abraham Kuyper argued that Christians are not up against individual theories but comprehensive worldviews. The only sure defense is to frame Christianity as an equally comprehensive worldview. Only then will genetic Just-So stories be relegated to the storybooks, where they belong.

## Mad Advertising

Another subverting influence on absolute morality is contemporary advertising. Commercials are cultural bellwethers. Advertisers spend fortunes on studies to probe our psyches so they can pitch their products to our deepest longings. They have learned that it is profitable to exploit Americans' growing spiritual hunger.

There is no missing the religious overtones in this familiar television commercial of a few years back: with a flood threatening to wash away the family home, a father cries out for help. Behold, the heavens open and a giant cartoon hand descends to rescue the family from disaster. The company, of course, is Allstate Insurance. One almost expects to see the family offer up a prayer: "We thank thee, Allstate, for thy help in times of trouble."

The need for salvation has been imprinted on the human soul since the Fall. Ironically, in contemporary America, advertisers seem to be more attuned to that need than our spiritual leaders are, and more adept at exploiting it.

This is no accident: the spiritual sequence of sin-guilt-redemption is transposed into the psychological sequence of problem-anxiety-resolution. We see a man or woman in distress: he has a cold; she has stains on the laundry. A second figure appears on the screen promising relief. This person gives witness to the power of the featured product. The product is tried and, hallelujah! the problem is solved. Finally, the disembodied voice of a male announcer—like a voice from on high—presses home the product's advantages. The allure of religion and advertising is the same, says sociologist James Twitchell. Both reassure us: "We will be rescued."

The goal of advertising, novelist John Updike writes, is "to persuade us that a certain beer or candy bar, or insurance company, or oil-based conglomerate, is, like the crucified Christ . . . the gateway to the good life." In other words, modern advertising is selling us more than just a product. Today's commercials offer a material solution to our spiritual longings.

This is another step in the process of subverting the Christian concept of absolutes. Our immediate, personal wants become existential needs, and as needs they become paramount over any restricting concept of right or wrong. I have a right to satisfy my deepest need in any way that makes me feel good. Advertising tells us that our immediate material wants should not be thwarted, for they are, after all, the easy answer at hand for our deepest desires. The absolute is replaced by the immediate.

Of course, commercials have always sold more than products. A few years ago, Saab launched their "Find your own road" campaign featuring characters who fantasize about never shaving again, about leaving work, about "flying in the face of convention," and driving off into the sunset. In other words, Saab wasn't just selling cars, it was selling a philosophy: the theme of autonomy, of breaking the rules, of rebellion against the constraints of civilized society.

When an ad features a well-dressed businessman, it's selling an image of success. When an ad features a sultry model, well, we all know what it's selling. But it is profoundly disturbing to see religion reduced to one more handle for manipulating viewers' acquisitive desires. When our kids hum the catchy jingle of the latest commercial, is their spiritual impulse being diverted into consumerism? Are they absorbing Madison Avenue's false values?

We must remember that no part of our postmodern culture is religiously neutral, no part free from the need for an informed Christian critique. Ads do a service when they convey information about a product in a creative manner. But today's ads often do much more: they exploit our deepest longings, sell false philosophies, pander to self-indulgence. And override our sense of moral absolutes.

## The End of Postmodernism

However, even with all this persuasive science and subversive advertising that pervades our society, there are signs that postmodernism is losing strength. According to a 2010 Gallup Poll, kids aren't inheriting the attitudes of their pro-choice (and horrified) parents. Instead, they are reflecting national trends showing that among eighteen- to twenty-nine-year-olds, support for legalized abortion dropped from 28 percent in 2000 to 24 percent in 2010. This number contrasts sharply with that of 1975 when only 18 percent of young adults said abortion should be illegal.[3] Clearly, this generation, witnessing the dreadful legacy of abortion, isn't buying pro-choice claims.

In recent years, Americans have become increasingly tolerant of homosexual rights. But in the wake of the Supreme Court's 2003 *Lawrence* decision, which many believe paved the way for so-called "gay marriage" to become the issue of the day, support for gay causes dropped sharply. Why? Because while it was fashionable to consider ourselves tolerant, *Lawrence* jolted many of us back to reality—back to an understanding of how destructive it will be if we overturn the definition of marriage as a union between one man and one woman.

Soccer moms—a constituency that worried about abortion rights, good schools, and civil liberties, are now called security moms because these days they worry primarily about their kids' safety. *Time* magazine quoted one mother who said she normally chooses political candidates who strongly support welfare and abortion. But since September 11, she said, "All I want in a president is a person who is strong."

September 11, the eminent theologian Michael Novak says, was the beginning of the end for postmodern preeminence. On that day people began to realize postmodern presuppositions simply don't work. And what are those presuppositions? That there are no absolutes—no absolute morality, no absolute truth. All claims to morality or truth are merely personal preferences, and to claim that they are absolute is merely an attempt to impose your preferences on others before they impose theirs on you.

But then came September 11, the day terrorists imposed *their* preferences, murdering 3,000 innocent people. If one's worldview is true, it has to conform to reality—to our real-life experiences. After September 11, few Americans could continue believing that there's no such thing as moral truth, no such thing as good and evil.

## SPEAKING TO POSTMODERNS

These encouraging signs—that Americans are recognizing the flimsiness of postmodernism's presuppositions—afford a great opportunity. I believe people today can be attracted to a belief system that is rational and defensible. The question is, who or what will fill the vacuum if postmodernism collapses?

Christianity offers a belief system that is, as Paul tells Festus, "true and reasonable." I can't think of a more critical time for pastors, scholars, and laypeople to be grounded in a biblical worldview and to defend it clearly to those hungering for truth.

But are we prepared for such a challenge? A George Barna tour of American churches led him to the dismaying conclusion that most church and lay leaders—90 percent, according to one survey—have no understanding of worldview. How are we going to contend with competing philosophies if we're not even rooted in our own truth system?

Ironically, just as there seem to be encouraging signs in the culture, there are also signs that the church is dumbing down, moving from a Word-driven message to an image- and emotion-driven message (note how many Christian radio stations have converted from talk and preaching to all music).

It would be the supreme irony—and a terrible tragedy—if we found ourselves slipping into postmodernity just when the broader culture has figured out it's a dead end. Yet, that very thing is happening. "Don't fight postmodernity," one speaker, a popular theologian, exhorted a packed crowd of Christian educators. "Take advantage of it. Express experience over reason, image over words."

But the man is seriously mistaken. Postmodernism must be fought. It has rejected not only God and reason but also the very idea of universally valid truth. It teaches that individuals are locked in the limited perspective of their own race, sex, or ethnic group; claims to moral truth are viewed as oppressive. Postmodernism has thus radically altered the way many in this generation think about life's most basic suppositions.

Admittedly, as postmoderns begin filling our pews, we have a communication problem. It becomes increasingly hard for those who think in traditional terms to communicate the biblical view of life, or even to present the gospel. When we speak of truth—meaning binding absolutes—our postmodern neighbors hear just one more opinion among many. The biblical story, which we present as divine revelation, is seen merely as one of many, equally valid cultural narratives.

This makes moral propositions increasingly problematic to postmodern listeners. For instance, how can we argue for the "common good" when postmodernists don't believe in a common good, seeking instead, as philosopher John Gray put it, merely "to reconcile conflicting goods"?

We lack even a common language for moral discourse. When we use the term *liberty*, for example, we mean the classic definition, famously articulated by Benjamin Franklin: the right to do what is right. Our Founders tied freedom—the highest political goal—to moral truth. But when newcomers to our pews hear the word *liberty*, they think the definition is "the unrestricted right to do what one pleases." They do not realize that moral absolutes are our only guarantee of freedom. Without transcendent moral truths above individual preferences, human rights founder.

What we're witnessing is the fulfillment of Nietzsche's formulation: "languages of good and evil" are rooted in neither truth nor reason, but in the will to power. The vacuum of postmodernity means whoever is in power decides right and wrong. On its face, that's bad news for Christians as well as for the liberty that postmoderns demand.

So how do we engage the postmodern mind?

Some Christians—like that conference speaker—think we should join the postmodern bandwagon's emphasis on experience. One pastor told me that ten years ago he could discuss moral truth with unbelievers, while "today I connect only on grounds of pain and compassion." But connecting only at the level of feelings is a weak reed for evangelism. Someone might "feel" right about Christianity—until those feelings change. And even a person who is drawn to Christ existentially has no context in which to understand those beliefs or the church's moral teachings. Significantly, a recent Barna poll revealed that the most common basis for moral decision-making among Christians is "doing whatever feels right" in a given situation. This is why, sadly, Christians and non-Christians divorce at the same rate.

Postmodernism must be confronted, not accommodated. We must challenge its false presuppositions, lovingly explaining that there is truth and that it is knowable.

To reach today's culture, seminarians, pastors, and laity, not unlike foreign missionaries, must learn to translate for today's postmoderns. For example, if we say, "The truth shall make you free," it means one thing to us—truth, that is Christ, makes us free from sin and death. But to the postmodern ear, it means "my preference" will make me free—to do whatever I want. Without translation, this becomes an invitation to cheap grace in the extreme.

That conference speaker was wrong. We dare not embrace postmodernism. The gospel is not a matter of soothing feelings or rewarding experiences (although it may produce both). It is the Truth that postmodernists can stake their lives on.

# 3

# Bringing Sanity to Moral Confusion

# 3

# Bringing Sanity
## to Moral Confusion

Few would argue that there has been a significant change in America's thinking about moral truth.[1] That change became apparent in the wake of three incidents that we witnessed in the last two decades. Similar or perhaps worse incidents may have occurred since, but I mark these three as signposts signaling America's reversal in its attitude toward moral truth. These incidents did not cause the change, but they revealed in letters too bold to be ignored that such a change had occurred.

The first incident was the Oval Office sexual escapades of President Clinton in the late 1990s. The Clinton scandals taught us much more about ourselves than about President Clinton. It was as though America woke up one morning and saw a different face in the mirror—like Dorian Gray looking at his portrait—and suddenly realized its own character had drastically altered.

One thing became clear: this was not the America we once thought it to be. The values that historically shaped our country's moral consciousness had been shattered. Two-thirds of

Americans said the nation's chief law-enforcement officer had committed perjury—but so what? He was only covering up a sexual relationship.

Those saying this were boomers who grew up during the sexual revolution, which taught "that sex is at the core of our identity and that sexual self-expression is critical to personal authenticity," according to Katherine Kersten of the Center of the American Experiment. "To suggest that sex has a moral component—to make value judgments—is to impede life's central task of unfettered 'self-actualization.'"

The second incident that exposed our moral sea change was the scandalous collapse of the Enron Corporation in late 2001, caused by unscrupulous accounting practices which cost innocent investors billions of dollars. Even before the dust settled on the Enron eruption—the biggest bankruptcy in American history—regulators, legislators, and prosecutors were sifting through the rubble seeking an explanation for such a massive ethical collapse. How could the auditors have been so negligent? Was there no way to safeguard against this in the future? What new regulations were needed?

These were important questions. But the most crucial questions were ones secular observers seemed unwilling to ask: Was Enron merely a symptom of something deeply wrong with our society? Had value-free postmodernity, the fruit of modern secularism, undermined the moral foundation essential for democratic capitalism?

The third example of our ethical slippage was the exposure in 2005 of former FBI deputy director Mark Felt as the long-secret Watergate source known as "Deep Throat." This revelation revived the 1970s political drama of Watergate: movies were being produced, books published, and Watergate revisited on talk shows.

As one of the few Watergate survivors, I appeared on dozens of programs. "Is Mark Felt a hero?" I was repeatedly asked. My answer was emphatically *No*. He broke the law to pursue his (presumably) noble objective of bringing down a corrupt administration. But the question that should have been asked regarding Mark Felt was whether he had no other recourse than to break the law. The answer is clearly no. He didn't need to: instead of sneaking around at night giving highly classified FBI information to reporters, he could have confronted the president, or, if the president refused to hear him, he could have gone to Congress or held a press conference. (Those who accuse me of rewriting history—who say that Felt could not possibly have confronted the president—forget that I worked in the inner sanctum of the White House; I know if Felt had spoken out, Nixon would have had to straighten out the mess or see his presidency fall a year earlier.)

Following the interviews, I received an avalanche of angry mail. *Of course* Felt was a hero, my correspondents insisted, as did all but one of the television interviewers. In the rush to canonize Felt, no one asked if he did the right thing. Did the end justify the means?

I understand why Felt wanted to stop Watergate. In my book, *The Good Life*, I confess I should have acted to stop the spreading scandal. One night, when, in my presence, Nixon ordered H. R. (Bob) Haldeman to get a team in place for break-ins, I should have spoken up: "No, Mr. President, you can't do that." But I rationalized: we were at war, Marine classmates of mine were in combat, and the Cold War hung in the balance. Maybe the president had to take extreme steps.

I now realize that we humans have an infinite capacity for self-justification: "The heart is deceitful above all things." So knowing what was right, I did what was wrong and justified myself in the process. I employed wrong means for what I perceived to be good ends, and I was sentenced to prison (ironically, for giving *one* FBI file to a reporter).

Today, I'm less concerned about how history judges Felt or Nixon (or me) than I am about the message that was sent to this generation by the general reaction to the morality of Felt's act. If we teach them that the end justifies the means, almost anything up to and including the Holocaust can be justified. As with any principle, there are exceptions, of course—as when Corrie ten Boom lied to German soldiers about hiding Jews. Churchill said sometimes the truth is so precious that it must be accompanied by a bodyguard of lies. In wartime, there may be no choice.

I fear that what the public reaction to the exposure of Mark Felt reveals is the revival of Machiavellian philosophy—the idea that one can do whatever it takes to gain his ends. In only three decades, we have erased the greatest moral lesson of that scandal—that no one is above the law—and replaced it with the Machiavellian lesson that anything goes.

## The Abdication of Moral Responsibility

As these three incidents show, somewhere along the way our nation has succumbed to the ravages of relativism and lost the adherence to absolute moral truth that held sway for the first two hundred years of our republic. We can't say we weren't warned. In the early nineties, theologian Michael Novak argued that Western liberal democracy is like a three-legged stool. Political freedom is the first leg, economic freedom the second, and moral responsibility the third. Weaken any leg, and the stool topples.

Public reaction to President Clinton's dalliance and lying, Enron's collapse, and Mark Felt's end-run around the law all expose a decayed third leg. We would not be able to point to these incidents as evidence of decaying ethics if they had been committed by thugs or obscure people. But they were not. They were committed by well-educated people in highly visible and responsible positions. Enron, for example, was not some sleazy, backroom bucket shop, mind you; it involved the best and brightest, pillars of the community. Enron Chairman Kenneth Lay boasted that he hired only graduates of the top business schools like Harvard and Wharton.

But we shouldn't be surprised. In the late eighties, I argued, somewhat impertinently, that Harvard couldn't teach ethics because it was committed to philosophical relativism. Irritated Harvard trustees invited me to give a lecture at the business school, which I provocatively titled "Why Harvard Can't Teach Ethics." I expected a riot after my forty-five-minute talk in a packed lecture hall. But the students were docile; I didn't hear a single good question. Were the students so unfamiliar with moral philosophy they didn't know enough to challenge me?

I left Harvard worried. What would happen to these students when they became leaders of American business? The answer came little over a decade later: one of the students at Harvard during that period was Jeffrey Skilling, the now-discredited former Enron CEO. Enron's collapse again exposed the glaring failure of the academy. Ethics historically rests on absolute truth, which our educational institutions have systematically assaulted for four decades.

## MORAL CONFUSION IN OUR COURTS

The decaying of moral and ethical absolutes in our nation becomes even more alarming when we realize that it is occurring even in our courts of law. If we expect protection from the fallout of ethical erosion from our judges and justices, we may be disappointed. Many Christians haven't noticed, but the idea that civil law should be based on a moral law has lost ground on both sides of the ideological divide.

To illustrate the point, a Supreme Court justice said recently, "If the people want abortion, the state should permit abortion in a democracy." Sound like one of the liberal justices? Not so: it was the conservative jurist Antonin Scalia. Scalia's remarks were made in an unpublished speech at Gregorian University where he argued that moral law has no place in formulating court opinions. In a democracy the majority rules, Scalia said—"and the minority loses, except to the extent that the majority . . . has agreed to accord the minority rights."

*This* is conservative legal theory? Hardly. It's pure majoritarianism. Scalia believes in a higher law, a natural law; but he insists that the people must write morality into the civil law through the legislature. Judges merely interpret the text—without consulting morality, tradition, or even legislative intent.

Among liberal judges, morally rooted legislation has always been a favorite target. For example, in *Edwards v. Aguillard* (1997), the Court rejected a statute requiring balanced treatment of evolution and creation, despite supporters' claims that it achieved a secular purpose (academic freedom). Justice William Brennan noted the "parallel" between creation and biblical teaching and denounced the proposed secular purpose as a "sham." What are we to conclude? Is any law that parallels biblical teaching invalid no matter how socially beneficial?

In *Lee v. Weismann* (1992), Justice Anthony Kennedy said it is impermissible not only for religion to inform the law but also for any "ethic and morality which transcends human invention." In *Romer v. Evans* (1996), Justice Kennedy decreed that a law barring special civil rights for sexual orientation implied an "animus," or hostility, against homosexuals. In short, a law informed by a religious or transcendent morality represents not a principled conviction but an ugly prejudice—and must be struck down.

These cases represent a striking departure from the entire history of Western civilization. Since the ancient Greeks, the law was understood to be a codification of a people's moral tradition, resting ultimately on divine law. English common law, which we inherited, reflects that belief: "The law of nature dictated by God Himself is binding in all countries and at all times," wrote the great English jurist William Blackstone.

But this great tradition is now being abandoned. And Christians are caught in the jaws of a vise: on one side, conservatives like Justice Scalia say the courts may not consult morality, that it's up to the people to encode morality into the law through the legislation. On the other side, liberals like Justice Kennedy say Christian morality may not be encoded into the law because it is nothing but prejudice, and Justice Brennan denounced Christian efforts to shape a just social order as a "sham."

As much as we would like to think we can rely on the traditions and wisdom of our judicial system to provide a firewall against the rising moral confusion of our day, it has become apparent that even our courts are now infected with the disease.

## PURVEYORS OF IMMORALITY

America's moral confusion is further demonstrated in the hypocrisy of our efforts to export freedom to other nations. One vital goal of the war in Iraq, and the war against terrorism, is to bring democracy to the heart of the Islamic world. Our hope is to make freedom so attractive that other Muslim countries will follow suit. But when radical Islamists see American women abusing Muslim men, as they did in the Abu Ghraib prison, and when they see news coverage of same-sex couples being "married" in U.S. towns, we make our kind of freedom abhorrent—something they see as a blot on Allah's creation.

As *Christianity Today* managing editor Mark Galli wrote soon after September 11, Islamic militants are angry at the West for exporting "hedonism and materialism into their very homes through television, enticing Muslims to become religiously lazy and morally corrupt." Galli quoted a 1985 communiqué from the terrorist group Hezbollah: "Our way is one of radical combat against depravity, and America is the original root of depravity."

Anger at Western decadence fueled the writings of the radical Sayyid Qutb, which so influenced Osama bin Laden. These people see themselves not as terrorists, but as holy warriors fighting a holy war against decadence. When we tolerate trash on television, permit pornography to invade our homes via the Internet, and allow babies to be killed at the point of birth, we are inflaming radical Islam and shutting down any possibility of their becoming open to our attempts to export democracy. They are all too well aware of what we are exporting; moral corruption. Sadly, it seems our adversaries may understand the truth about us better than we do.

## RESTORING MORAL SANITY

Is all hope lost for America? Have we gone so far down the road toward moral confusion that our momentum will carry us over the precipice into chaos and oblivion? It does not have to be so. Just as God would have saved Sodom and Gomorrah for the sake of ten righteous men, I believe he can heal and save America if Christians will begin to live their calling actively. I see three things Christians can do to turn the ship around.

The first is to address the urgent need for our lawmakers and judges to pass and interpret state and national laws in conformance with natural law. The challenge is to understand that the forces of postmodernity have emboldened those hostile to any moral influence in the law. The time has come for Christians not only to focus on individual issues of public policy but also to revive a comprehensive philosophy of the law that articulates the role of religious and moral truth in the public arena.

The law, Augustine and Aquinas postulated, is the codification of the people's moral consensus informed by revelation. For centuries, this conviction prevailed in the West and inspired respect for the law. Blackstone wrote, "This law of nature [is] dictated by God himself ... no laws are of any validity if contrary to this"—a view echoed by Martin Luther King Jr. in his "Letter from a Birmingham Jail."

In Western democracies, the people, through their representatives, can ensure that the law reflects their moral traditions. But as we have noted, today's courts have increasingly attacked those morally based visions of the common good. Government (usually in the person of activist courts) today sees its role as protecting people from any "imposition" of moral truth. But the law separated from its moral moorings becomes tyranny.

This trend can be arrested if Christians become diligent in instigating a healthy national debate. Ongoing debate can sensitize the president and governors to appoint judges who will *interpret* and not *make* laws. And judges do pay attention to public opinion. Aware of disabled demonstrators protesting on its steps in 1997, the Court stepped back from the precipice and affirmed Washington state's ban on assisted suicide. The imperial presidency was dethroned in the 1970s by mobs marching in the streets of Washington protesting Vietnam and Watergate. To dethrone the imperial judges calls for, if not public marches, at least similar outrage.

If we do not act now, we will see our constitutional order crumble, while we ourselves are steadily driven to the margins, wondering why we feel like strangers in our own land.

Second, Christians must contend for the biblical worldview in the economic marketplace. Examine the roots of the Western free market, and we see the profound influence of Judeo-Christian revelation. Scripture endorses concepts like private property, contract rights, rule of law, and the discharge of debts—all essential to free markets. The Bible also demands justice, warning of God's judgment against oppressors who withhold wages or take advantage of the needy; it condemns those who manipulate the economy, whether by greed, hoarding, indolence, or deception. The command to permit gleaning—allowing the poor to harvest crops along the borders of farms—shows us how a biblical welfare system works. The scriptural system, in short, balances the acquisition of wealth with a demand for both justice and compassion, and requires people to subordinate self-interest to moral demands.

Through the centuries, Christians have fought to do just that, opposing exploitation of workers by the powerful and bringing biblical justice into the marketplace. Nineteenth-century England affords a good example. Following rapid industrialization, conditions in the factories were deplorable. Children as young as seven were forced to work twelve hours daily. Women and children labored in coal mines. The great Christian statesman Lord Shaftesbury, who famously argued that "what is morally wrong cannot be politically right," led a crusade against these conditions, exposing what poet William Blake called "the dark Satanic mills." The crusade was so successful that an economics historian would later write that Shaftesbury "did more than any other single man in English history to check the raw power of the new industrial system."

The lesson of history is that capitalism (or any other economic system, for that matter) is beneficent only when it is subject to moral restraints derived ultimately from religious truth. These same moral restraints have been dangerously loosened, as Enron revealed. The resulting chaos can only lead to deadening bureaucratic regulations—and, inevitably, the loss of freedom. Unless, that is, we rebuild the third leg of Michael Novak's stool. This will require a heroic effort but it's one that Christians are uniquely equipped to undertake.

Third, Christians must find a new way of communicating the vital necessity of adhering to absolute moral and ethical standards. What we saw in the public's failure to be outraged by President Clinton's sexual escapades and lying was not a mere "loosening" of sexual morality, it was a sea change, the embrace of an entirely new moral philosophy—and one exceedingly resistant to rational critique. In the past, one might have challenged a moral point through reasoned argument, appealing to commonly accepted standards of right and wrong. Today, however, as I have discovered lecturing on campuses, young people have never been exposed to moral philosophy but are indoctrinated instead into a perspective that treats morality as one of many strategies for self-development.

The upshot is that rational arguments no longer work. So how do we make a difference? How do we affect moral sensibilities? Several years ago over lunch, my friend Bill Bennett suggested that people today are all but impervious to moral philosophy and are more likely to be moved by moral literature. His point was proved when his *The Book of Virtues*, a collection of classic moral stories, became a megahit.

Later came more books from other authors with a similar purpose, such as Vigan Guroian's *Tending the Heart of Virtue: How*

*Classic Stories Awaken a Child's Imagination.* And for adults, Os Guinness and Louise Cowan have edited *Invitation to the Classics,* essays by fifty Christian scholars on classic literature.

These authors are on to something, pointing perhaps to an important way for Christians to engage the culture—by appealing to the moral imagination through classic literature. Stories change us because they reach the whole person, not just the cognitive faculty. As we read, we identify with characters who demonstrate courage and self-sacrifice, vicariously making choices along with them—and in the process, our own character is shaped. As C. S. Lewis writes, "I become a thousand men, yet remain myself."

Many classics were composed by great Christian writers and can even help draw people to faith. Louise Cowan tells how she lost her childhood faith while in university religion courses— only to regain it later in literature courses. Tracing the Christian themes in Shakespeare spoke to her heart in a way that discursive theological treatises failed to do. I too have gained from Dostoevsky's novels many of my deepest convictions about ethics, crime, sin, and grace.

So if we don't like the image of America we're seeing in the mirror, a good place to start is by changing ourselves: read the classics and stimulate our own moral imagination. Then read them to our children, and pass them on to our friends. Maybe we should rethink our strategy in the culture war as well. Instead of hurling rhetorical grenades, we should support programs for reading the classics in schools, getting people to think about enduring moral and spiritual themes. For too long many Christians have tried to have an impact through political activism alone. The lesson of the scandals of the last two or three decades is that the nation's wound runs much deeper than politics. Politics is an expression of a culture, merely a reflection of America's own values. We must find ways to change those values, and Christians are uniquely equipped for the task.

Our model should be the church after the fall of the Roman Empire: the monks carefully guarded every book they could get their hands on, whether Christian theology or Greek and Roman philosophy and literature, and then taught them to the barbarians. It was the monasteries that preserved the best of the past and then gradually recivilized Europe.

More important than the outcome of the next election is the preservation of the riches of our literary and intellectual heritage so we can recivilize the modern barbarians living around us. As G. K. Chesterton wrote, "Any man who is cut off from the past . . . is a man most unjustly disinherited." Moreover, when a culture's history is neglected, says Donald Drew in *Human Events*, "its sign-posts and landmarks disappear," and it loses its sense of direction. As the country wrestles with its moral identity, Christians have an opportunity to help it regain its moral direction, and literature may be one of the best landmarks we can offer.

# 4

# ADDRESSING
# SEXUAL DIS-INTEGRATION

# 4

# Addressing
# Sexual Dis-integration

The newspaper photo showed two men kissing as their friends joyously threw rice.[1] Unbelievably, it was their wedding day—and their "marriage" was, thanks to a Canadian court, as legal as any heterosexual marriage. Not long afterward, this Canadian infection of marital and legal confusion spread across the border into the United States, creating havoc in our courts and legislatures.

It all started on June 11, 2004, when a Canadian appeals court ruled unconstitutional Canada's ban on so-called "homosexual marriage." Within hours, the first same-sex Canadian couple rushed into matrimony. Three weeks later, in *Lawrence v. Texas*, the U.S. Supreme Court ruled six to three that sodomy is protected behavior under the Constitution's so-called "right to privacy" provision. Gays hailed the decision as the prelude to homosexual "marriage" in America—and they were right. It was the prelude, as well, to legally sanctioned polygamy, incest, pedophilia, and bestiality. As Justice Antonin Scalia angrily roared in dissent, the decision "effectively decrees the end of all morals legislation."

This is precisely the point Senator Rick Santorum and Alabama Attorney General Bill Pryor (who had at that time been nominated for the Circuit Court) were vilified for making. Radical gays and the media falsely claimed Santorum equated homosexual behavior with bestiality and incest. Nonsense. He was simply stating the obvious: if the Court sanctioned sodomy on privacy grounds, it would then have no rationale for outlawing other private, consensual sexual acts.

How, for example, could we then continue to uphold laws against polygamy? After all, a polygamist and his wives engage in private, consensual sex. So does a father who wants to sleep with his consenting teenage daughter—or son. Ditto the man who engages in bestiality, for, according to ethicist Peter Singer, animals can give nonverbal consent.

This was the dirty little secret behind *Lawrence v. Texas*—which is why the gay lobby so viciously attacked anyone who exposed it. Americans may tolerate sodomy—but most draw the line at incest, polygamy, and bestiality.

These and subsequent court and legislative actions raise the question: is America witnessing the end of marriage? In 2003 the Supreme Judicial Court of Massachusetts ordered that the state issue marriage licenses to same-sex couples. (By spring of 2004, the Massachusetts legislature voted to recognize same-sex civil unions instead.) An unprecedented period of municipal lawlessness followed, with officials in California, New York, Oregon, and New Mexico gleefully mocking their state constitutions and laws by passing legislation allowing gays to wed. The result: thousands of gays rushed to these municipalities to "marry," while much of the news media egged them on. Subsequent elections, legislation, referendums, and court decisions negated these laws or put them on hold, throwing the whole issue into chaos. At this writing, the final outcome is uncertain. President Obama instructed the Justice Department in February 2011 to no longer defend the Defense of Marriage Act, or DOMA—the legal prohibition on federal recognition of so-called same-sex marriages—while Congress and a growing number of state legislatures seem determined to stop the legalization of so-called gay marriage.

The issue—and the confusion it spreads—was debated way back in 1996 when the sitcom *Friends* ran a segment featuring a lesbian wedding. After the broadcast, a clergyman lectured readers of a Missouri newspaper who might be opposed to gay marriage to grow up and learn a little "openness." "The issue," he wrote, is "learning to live in a multicultural, multi-mores, multi-religious, multi-everything world." When even some religious leaders push for so-called same-sex marriage, we shouldn't wonder that it is a burning cultural issue today.

## The Underlying Problem

How did America fall into this quagmire of confusion? In the previous chapter I pegged the public reaction to President Clinton's sexual indiscretions with White House intern Monica Lewinsky as a marker showing the radically changed sexual attitudes in our country. Instead of the nation as a whole being appalled, the president's approval ratings soared with each new accusation. In an NBC/*Wall Street Journal* poll, a whopping 66 percent said the president should not be impeached even if the accusations prove true. Man-in-the-street interviews revealed a general indifference.

Even the usually indignant feminists opined that since the alleged sexual relationship was consensual, it is no big deal.

This public reaction astounded many of us because it revealed just how deeply American attitudes toward sexual immorality had sunk. How could so many shrug off such charges? I put the question to Robert George, professor of political philosophy at Princeton University. His answer not only revealed why we have become so sexually confused that affairs and adultery don't raise our moral hackles; it articulated basic principles that reveal the underlying problem of homosexuality and the push to legalize so-called homosexual marriage. It reveals why the populace is slipping into a mode of thinking in which they can believe anything goes sexually.

"It's because they've lost a sense of the sacredness of human life," Dr. George replied.

"I'm not talking about abortion," I said, puzzled. "I'm talking about adultery."

"Both derive from the same worldview," he explained. Modern secular orthodoxy splits the human being, dividing the person from the body. The body is treated as an instrument for getting what the self wants—pleasure, emotional satisfaction, whatever.

This may sound abstract, but the consequences of a person/body dualism are painfully concrete. It follows that the body is not really "me" but something other than my real self—something like a possession to be deployed or disposed of. Thus abortion: secularists insist that a human embryo is merely a body, not a full person, and can be readily discarded. Thus assisted suicide: secularists who decide the body is giving them too much pain or bother may opt for suicide—and even demand that a physician help out. Thus sex outside marriage or homosexual connections: the sexual union of two bodies does not necessarily mean the union of two persons on all levels of their being (marriage), but only that two selves are using their bodies for mutual pleasure or affection.

We will not understand the secular position on these contentious moral issues unless we grasp the underlying person/body dualism. The idea that sex outside marriage or homosexual connections is morally okay implies that the body is merely a vehicle for getting what you want—just as you use a car to get where you want to go.

This runs totally against the grain of the Christian worldview. Since the apostles, the church has opposed dualist heresies. We believe that God created each individual as a unity—body, soul, and spirit. At the end of time, our bodies will be raised to life eternal. We affirm this whenever we recite the Apostles' Creed: "I believe . . . in the resurrection of the body." Christianity grants the body extraordinary dignity. What we do with our bodies expresses who we are as full persons. We utterly reject any dualism that breaks up the individual and relegates the body to a merely instrumental role.

This explains why God speaks so strongly against homosexuality and sex outside marriage. Sexual unity is a unity of two whole persons. That's how we were made. If we engage in sex outside marriage—if we form a bodily union apart from a union of whole persons—we violate our wholeness. That is to say, we violate our integrity (which literally means wholeness). We disintegrate ourselves. That's why sex outside marriage is so devastating: it shatters the integrity of our being.

How does this apply to so-called gay marriage? As both Catholic and Protestant philosophers have noted, "gay marriage" is the ultimate oxymoron. In his book *The Clash of Orthodoxies*, Dr. George writes that matrimonial law reflects both the biblical and natural law understandings that marriage is a two-in-one flesh communion of persons, consummated by acts that are reproductive in type, whether or not they result in children. They unite the spouses as a single procreative unit—an organic unity achieved even by infertile couples.

By contrast, Dr. George writes, homosexual acts have no relationship to procreation and can't unite persons organically. Thus, these acts cannot be marital—which means homosexual relationships cannot be marriages.

And as philosopher J. Budziszewski writes in his book *What We Can't Not Know*, "To call procreation the purpose of marriage is not arbitrary; alone among all forms of human union, the union of the sexes produces children. . . . A legislature [or a court] can no more turn sodomitical unions into marriages than it can turn dogs into cats; it can only unravel the institution of marriage by sowing confusion."

Tragically, our culture is *already* confused. A recent Gallup poll revealed that 40 percent of Americans, and 61 percent of younger Americans, think so-called same-sex marriages should be legal.

## THE PUSH TO LEGITIMIZE SO-CALLED GAY MARRIAGE

As we write, the courts are on a fast track to legalization, and the Supreme Court has already paved the way: in *Romer v. Evans*, it invalidated Colorado's referendum denying special legal protections to homosexuals, on the grounds that such laws create an "inevitable inference of animus." The logic of Romer could easily be used to define as bigotry any law against so-called gay marriage (not to mention polygamy and other deviations from the traditional norm).

While the courts have sped forward, legislatures have scrambled to put on the brakes. Many people are concerned that when so-called homosexual marriage is legalized in a given state, homosexuals will rush to that state to marry, then demand that their home states recognize their "marriages" (citing the Constitution's "full faith and credit" clause). While Congress rushed to pass the Defense of Marriage Act to prevent that from happening, several states have considered bills to limit marriage to male-female couples.

Yet on constitutional questions, the courts have the power to strike down state laws. If they do this, they will do little more than pave the way to a sexual free-for-all. They will codify cultural confusion about the very nature of marriage. If consensual sex of any kind is a constitutionally protected civil right, as Lawrence holds, the Equal Protection Clause should give gay couples the same right to formalize their relationships as heterosexual couples enjoy.

The only real hope for deterring the courts is through public opinion. Even today's liberal judges may be checked by an overwhelming democratic consensus. As Christians, we must help build a firewall in people's hearts and minds.

In the midst of the chaos, President Bush announced his support for a Federal Marriage Amendment, which assured that this contentious issue would be debated in every quarter of American life. It should be, because the consequences of having so-called gay marriage forced on us by judicial (or mayoral) fiat will fall on all Americans—not just those who embrace it. But the pro-gay "marriage" stand of the subsequent Obama administration dims any hope of White House support for such an amendment, so it is likely that the sexual confusion will continue for a while yet.

As a supporter of the amendment, I'm well aware of the critical arguments. As President Bush noted, "After more than two centuries of American jurisprudence, and millennia of human experience, a few judges and local authorities are presuming to change the most fundamental institution of civilization. Their action has created confusion on an issue that requires clarity."

## THE CONSEQUENCES OF CONFUSION

President Bush was right. We do need clarity on the issue of so-called gay marriage, especially concerning its consequences to the stability of our society. Here's the clarity: Marriage is the traditional building block of human society, intended both to unite couples and bring children into the world. Tragically, the sexual revolution led to the decoupling of marriage and procreation; so-called same-sex marriage would pull them completely apart, leading to an explosive increase in family collapse, out-of-wedlock births—and crime. How do we know this?

In nearly thirty years of prison ministry, I've witnessed the disastrous consequences of family breakdown—in the lives of thousands of delinquents. Dozens of studies confirm the evidence I've seen with my own eyes. Boys who grow up without fathers are at least twice as likely as other boys to end up in prison. Sixty percent of rapists and 72 percent of adolescent murderers never knew or lived with their fathers.

Even in the toughest inner-city neighborhoods, just 10 percent of kids from intact families get into trouble, but 90 percent of those from broken families do. Girls raised without a father in the home are five times more likely to become mothers while still adolescents. Children from broken homes have more academic and behavioral problems at school and are nearly twice as likely to drop out of high school.

Critics agree with this, but claim so-called gay marriage will not weaken heterosexual marriage. The evidence says they're wrong. Stanley Kurtz of the Hoover Institution writes: "It follows that once marriage is redefined to accommodate same-sex couples, that change cannot help but lock in and reinforce the very cultural separation between marriage and parenthood that makes so-called gay marriage conceivable to begin with." He cites Norway, where courts imposed so-called same-sex marriage in 1993—a time when Norwegians enjoyed a low out-of-wedlock birth rate. After the imposition of so-called same-sex marriage, Norway's out-of-wedlock birth rate shot up as the link between marriage and childbearing was broken and cohabitation became the norm.

So-called gay marriage supporters argue that most family tragedies occur because of broken *heterosexual* marriages—including those of many Christians. They are right. We ought to accept our share of the blame, repent, and clean up our own house. But the fact that we have badly served the institution of marriage is not a reflection on the institution itself; it is a reflection on us.

Clearly, as we noted above, our culture has severed the tie between marriage and its purposes: procreation and spousal unity. Even many Christians accept the notion that sex is intended primarily for pleasure. And if sex is merely recreational, what's the rationale for denying marriage to gay couples? If heterosexuals can legalize *their* "recreation," why shouldn't gays?

## WHAT CAN CHRISTIANS DO?

Christians have to regain the high moral ground, making—to our secular neighbors—the natural order arguments that define the purposes of sex as unitive and procreative, and marriage as the stable, one-man, one-woman institution in which to rear children. This means we will have to be just as critical of heterosexuals engaging in extramarital, recreational sex as we are of homosexual behavior.

In our sex-saturated society, Christians cannot simply proclaim that adultery and homosexuality are against the Bible and stop there. We will be accused of "imposing morality." Instead, we must explain the contradictory understandings of the human person.

And we must press upon people what is really at stake. First, a person/body dualism is radically dehumanizing. It provides the justification for a host of pernicious practices—not only guilt-free adultery and homosexual acts, but also abortion, fetal experimentation, euthanasia, assisted suicide, and disregard for human rights. These practices strip the body of its intrinsic dignity and treat it as a commodity to be used, managed, even disposed of to suit our desires.

Second, if we engage in these practices, we deceive ourselves by embracing a false view of human nature. We sever the body from the self, destroying our integrity, our wholeness. We experience dis-integration. If Americans truly understood what adultery and homosexuality do—that they lead to the dis-integration of the human being—they would not dismiss it so lightly.

Finally, we must constantly expose the secular myth that personal behavior has no effect on public morality. For the dis-integrated individual is incapable of forming and sustaining virtuous character, because the self abdicates moral control over the passions and impulses. And without character we cannot maintain relationships of trust, so that dis-integrated individuals in turn create dis-integrated communities.

This is what we are witnessing today: the chaos resulting from the controversy over so-called homosexual marriage in the courts, legislatures, and in public opinion should awaken us to the disastrous consequences of the modern secular worldview. That is something Americans cannot afford to shrug off.

To do that, we need to learn the language of public philosophy. In a post-Christian culture, simply quoting from the Bible doesn't cut any ice. In recent debates on the Hill, congressmen who quoted biblical verses prohibiting homosexuality were stereotyped as gay-bashers. Believers need to craft arguments understood by all citizens, translating biblical morality into statements about the public good.

Just how, then, does so-called gay marriage threaten the public good? Barney Frank, a gay congressman, phrased the question this way: "I don't understand how it hurts anybody else if two people want to be legally . . . responsible for each other."

His comment has a certain libertarian appeal, but it misses the point. Accepting homosexuals privately is not the same thing as normalizing homosexuality by granting homosexuals a legal right to the public institution of marriage.

Accepting same-sex relationships as the moral and legal equivalent of marriage will transform the very definition of marriage—with far-reaching repercussions. A society's view of marriage grows out of its worldview. In an article in *Crisis* magazine, the late David Coolidge of the Institute on Religion and Public Life once outlined two worldviews warring for dominance in America today.

The first Coolidge called the *Complementarity* model. As he explained, it assumes that the universe was created with an objective moral order, that the two sexes are part of that order, that marriage is the fundamental social institution by which we unite our lives in family and kinship relationships. This model is virtually universal in traditional societies; it underlies the marriage laws in all fifty states; and it is compatible with Christianity. In legal terms, the right to marry means the state's recognition of a prior moral order.

But that model has been challenged by what Coolidge called the *Choice* model. This worldview assumes that the universe is malleable and that individuals create their own truths, their own values. Sexuality has no intrinsic purpose; it is merely an opportunity for pleasure, intimacy, and reproduction. Family structure is as pliable as Play-Doh, and virtually any form is acceptable. Here the right to marry is no more than the right of individuals to participate in state-defined benefits.

These two models give us helpful categories for talking with nonbelievers even now. They also highlight what is at stake: if so-called same-sex marriage wins the day legally, it will exert enormous pressure throughout society to move from the *Complementarity* to the *Choice* model. The message will be built into the law itself that there is no objective moral order, that marriage is a human invention. And if people believe marriage is just an invention, then they will feel free to change it, redefine it, or even discard it. The *Choice* model would inevitably weaken men and women's commitment to the institution of marriage.

And the results would be tragic. Today the empirical evidence is undeniable that family breakdown feeds a host of social pathologies. It is the single most reliable predictor of school problems, teen pregnancy, chemical addictions, and crime. In *Life Without Father*, David Popenoe notes that 70 percent of long-term prison inmates grew up in fatherless homes.

This is the rationale Christians should be using in the public arena. Marriages are fragile enough today. Take away legal recognition of its unique status, and we are sure to see an even more rapid erosion of family life—with all its frightening consequences.

As we debate the wisdom of legalizing so-called gay marriage, we must remember that, like it or not, there is a natural moral order for the family. History and tradition—and the teachings of Jews, Muslims, and Christians—support the overwhelming empirical evidence: the family, led by a married mother and father, is the best available structure for both child-rearing and cultural health.

This is why, although some people will always pair off in unorthodox ways, society as a whole must never legitimize any form of marriage other than that of one man and one woman, united with intention of permanency and the nurturing of children. Marriage is not a private institution designed solely for the individual gratification of its participants. If we fail to protect the institution of marriage, we can expect not just more family breakdown, but also more criminals behind bars and more chaos in our streets. The stakes could not be higher.

# 5

## REVERSING
## CULTURAL DECAY

# 5

# REVERSING
# CULTURAL DECAY

In 1978 a fifty-nine-year-old bearded dissident, whose writings helped expose and eventually bring down Soviet tyranny, stood in Harvard's historic Yard facing rows of robed faculty and graduates at its 327th commencement.[1] Expectations ran high. Aleksandr Solzhenitsyn was admired for his literary achievements and lionized by the faculty, if not for his outspoken views on communism, at least for the fact that he was an oppressed intellectual.

Solzhenitsyn delivered each line in his high-pitched voice in Russian. The translation blunted the impact somewhat—in fact, there were even sporadic bursts of applause before the audience clearly understood the direction of the speech. But soon enough, outraged professors realized that Solzhenitsyn was charging them with complicity in the West's surrender to liberal secularism, the abandonment of its Christian heritage, and with all the moral horrors that followed.

As it happened, I recently was reading a tattered copy of

Solzhenitsyn's speech[2] at the same time I was studying Jeremiah in my devotions. I was struck by the chilling parallels between the dissident's words and Jeremiah's warning to the Israelites. For example, describing the Western worldview as "rationalistic humanism," Solzhenitsyn decried the loss of "our concept of a Supreme Complete Entity which used to restrain our passions and our irresponsibility." Man has become "the master of this world . . . who bears no evil within himself," he announced. "So all the defects of life" are attributed to "wrong social systems."

Solzhenitsyn also argued that this moral impoverishment had led to a debased definition of freedom that makes no distinction between "freedoms for good" and "freedoms for evil." Our founders, he reminded us, would scarcely have countenanced "all this freedom with no purpose" but for the "satisfaction of one's whims"; they demanded that freedom be granted conditionally upon the individual's constant exercise of his religious responsibility. Solzhenitsyn could hardly have imagined that just fourteen years later, the U.S. Supreme Court would enshrine this radical definition of freedom: "At the heart of liberty is the right to define one's own concept of existence, of the meaning of the universe, and of the mystery of human life."

Solzhenitsyn also foresaw the rise of political correctness: "Fashionable trends of thoughts and ideas are fastidiously separated from those that are not fashionable." He predicted this would lead to "strong mass prejudices" with people being "hemmed in by the idols of the prevailing fad."

Perhaps the hardest for the crowd to accept was his charge that the West had lost its "civic courage . . . particularly noticeable among the ruling and intellectual elites." After all, he said, with "unlimited freedom on the choice of pleasures," why should one risk one's precious life in defense of the common good, particularly when one's nation must be defended in distant lands? He even predicted Americans would care more about the rights of terrorists than their evil deeds—a prophecy fulfilled by the Supreme Court in *Boumediene v. Bush*, granting terror suspects access to U.S. courts—exactly thirty years to the week after Solzhenitsyn's speech.

The condition Solzhenitsyn diagnosed was identical to that of the ancient Israelites. God spoke through Jeremiah with biting sarcasm, warning the Israelites of where this kind of "freedom" leads: it would be freedom "to fall by the sword, plague and famine" (Jeremiah 34:17). Jeremiah's prophecy all too soon came to pass; the Israelites fell into Babylonian captivity.

Three decades after Solzhenitsyn's speech, where do Americans find themselves? In the grip of a similar captivity: a rapidly declining culture corrupted by violent and pornographic "entertainment," growing censorship of unfashionable ideas, and a spiritually exhausted citizenry.

## Signs of Disintegration

Today it is painfully clear that Solzhenitsyn's prophecies of America's cultural disintegration are coming to pass. We see clear evidence in many segments of culture, some directly related to his predictions and others in areas he did not address. Could even Solzhenitsyn have imagined that sexual rights would eventually triumph over free expression, that academia would impose rigid speech codes, or that churches would be threatened with loss of their tax-exempt status for opposing so-called homosexual marriage? Could he have imagined the extent of entertainment's descent into frank debauchery and overt sensationalism?

In the past decade, for example, Americans were introduced to a new sports sensation: XFL. Eighteen million people tuned in to NBC for the new football league's opening night in 2001. Considering all the players are NFL rejects, that was an astonishing figure; it was also a disquieting sign of the continued coarsening of American culture.

The X in XFL stood for extreme, as in extreme violence, sex, and "attitude." The "attitude" was the deliberate flouting of authority and convention. The games opened not with the traditional coin toss, but with a mad scramble for the ball, making it the only sport in which you could get knocked out before the game even started. Players openly used four-letter vulgarities—words easily recognizable despite being bleeped out.

Sex was big in the XFL. Buxom cheerleaders dispensed with pom-poms and plunged into the stands, dancing suggestively with fans while the TV cameras rolled. Adding vice to vulgarity, XFL founder Vince McMahon said he would ask cheerleaders if their sexual relationships with players were hampering the guys' performance on the field.

The XFL folded after one season—not because of its salacious and provocative content, but because it could not compete financially with the already well-established, highly popular, and highly profitable NFL. But the demise of the XFL has not stopped NBC and other major networks from airing highly sexualized programming that continually pushes the limits and lowers the standard for what the public will accept . . . and finally crave. Titillating bachelor and bachelorette series, so-called "reality" survival shows involving sexual tension, double-crossing, and ruthless competition among often ill-adjusted or socially deficient contestants draw voyeuristic viewers like flies to flypaper.

Ironically, the same week the XFL debuted, the Kaiser Family Foundation released findings from its study of sex on TV. The report said 68 percent of all primetime programming, and 84 percent of situation comedies, contained sexual content; 10 percent offer "strong suggestions" of sexual intercourse. Those figures have continued to increase, according to Foundation studies. Just four years later, 77 percent of all primetime shows included sexual content, averaging almost six sex scenes per hour.[3]

The degrading of our culture is nowhere more evident than in the parallel teen subculture that has been formed almost in isolation from adult supervision. Media executives whose one value is profit frankly pander decadence, rebellion, and narcissism to the immature tastes of juveniles who lack the discernment to understand the harm being done to them.

For contemporary teens, the highest value is simply being "cool." How do kids define *cool*? It's an amalgam of ideas fed to them by corporations that covet the $200 billion-a-year teen market.[4] These are the clothing manufacturers, media empires, and soft-drink companies that, as reported in the PBS documentary *The Merchants of Cool*, intentionally undermine cultural standards to market their wares to those wants.

And what do teenagers want? First, an adult-free universe—which is why TV programs marketed to teens feature so few adults (or when adults do appear, they are portrayed as buffoons or hypocrites). This, in turn, has become the model by which teenagers shape their own isolated culture. Leon Botstein, president of Baird College, characterizes American schools as "a gang in which individuals of the same age group define each other's world." Within this alternate universe, kids are free to determine not only hair and clothing styles, but also moral fashions: they decide the rules governing sexual behavior and drug and alcohol use. The classic novel *Lord of the Flies* warns what can happen when children live without adult guidance: they quickly descend into savagery. At least the children in William Golding's story didn't have adults pushing them into savagery, as real-life kids do. For, ironically, it is business-suited adults who support the parallel teen culture.

Second, teens want to see, on television and movie screens, what New York University's Douglas Rushkoff calls a "version of themselves." These versions are the templates for two TV stereotypes: "mooks" and "midriffs." The mook is a character created to appeal to adolescent males, characterized by "infantile, boorish behavior" and trapped in a state of "perpetual adolescence." Mooks are a staple on MTV. The midriff is, as Rushkoff describes her, a "highly sexualized, world-weary sophisticate" who manages to retain a bit of the little girl. Shows like MTV's raunchy (and recently canceled) soap *Skins* and singers like Britney Spears provide America's midriffs-in-training with role models to emulate.

Even more menacing are the McMorals taught by electronic game companies. Col. Dave Grossman, a former Army Ranger who researched the psychology of killing in combat, says violent video and computer games are conditioning teenagers to be violent. And then along comes Hollywood, telling kids through movies like *Teaching Mrs. Tingle*, *Urban Legend*, and *Scream IV* that violence and killing are cool.

Should anyone be surprised when kids act on these messages? We can and should get angry with the companies that through music and media market sex, antisocial behavior, anti-adult attitudes, provocative dress codes, and the glorification of violence to our children—but we should be just as angry at parents who allow their kids to become the companies' prey. The fact is, the parallel teen culture would be impossible without the complicity of parents. Many middle-class parents are so stressed from chauffeuring kids from one activity to another that they have little time together as a family. So today's teens enjoy unprecedented autonomy. We share the blame for schoolyard gangs, epidemic teen sex, rebellion against adult authority, and even school killings by allowing our kids to form a parallel culture almost completely free of adult supervision.

As dire as Solzhenitsyn's prophecies were, it's hard to imagine that even he could have envisioned how America's moral impoverishment would lead us to debase the use of our "freedoms for good" and allow marketing moguls to use those freedoms for evil, deliberately and openly undermining the morality, spirituality, and cultural development of the next generation.

Another evidence of the coarsening of our culture is found in our discourse. For example, news journals now defer to our sensitivities, not by omitting vulgarities, as they once did, but by using three dashes after the first letter of offensive words. Really clever. Over the water cooler at work or in school corridors, no one seems embarrassed anymore by conversations sprinkled with four-letter words.

Nowhere is the coarsening of our culture more evident than in our dress. I'm used to being an anachronism—the only person on an airplane wearing a coat and tie. Yes, I know business is going casual. But T-shirts stretched over protruding bellies, shorts exposing hairy legs, and toes sprouting out of sandals are not casual—they're slovenly. And you see it more and more on airplanes, in restaurants, and even in church.

You may be wondering why I am addressing such "minor" things as foul language and sloppy dress when our culture is facing a major breakdown in the much more critical areas I've already addressed, such as the disintegrating teen culture and the rampant violence and immorality in our sensationalized entertainment. I urge you to read on. I think you will see that these small things may give us a critical key to understanding the larger ones. When we begin to get slothful—to loosen our attention to the importance of smaller things, the slothfulness will spread like an infection into more important areas.

How we present ourselves to others says something about how we view ourselves. When I was a Marine, we checked our spit-shined shoes and starched khakis in a full-length mirror before leaving the barracks; it was drilled into us that if we were to be sharp we had to look sharp. That's the right kind of pride, the antidote to sloth.

The sin of sloth, as the late British journalist Henry Fairlie wrote in *The Seven Deadly Sins,* is "a state of dejection that gives rise to torpor of mind and feeling and spirit; to a sluggishness . . . a poisoning of the will; to despair, faintheartedness, and even desirousness . . . even for what is good. . . . Sloth is a deadly sin."

As Solzhenitzyn's speech pointedly asserted, we have arrived at this state. How did we get here from the high ideals affirmed and practiced by our founding fathers and early generations?

In his *A Study of History*, the great historian Arnold Toynbee contends that one clear sign of a civilization's decline is when elites—people Toynbee labels the "dominant minority"—begin mimicking the vulgarity and promiscuity exhibited by society's bottom-dwellers. This is precisely what some political leaders and most media moguls have done. The result: the entire culture is vulgarized.

If the connection between sloth and cultural deterioration seems vague or unlikely to you, consider the following stories: police in Newport News, Virginia, were weary of answering calls about burglars and drug dealers in a rundown housing project. Finally, the project was scheduled for demolition, and in preparation for the new construction, police decided to clean up the area: they carted away trash, removed abandoned cars, filled in potholes.

To everyone's surprise, as soon as the housecleaning began, burglary rates dropped 35 percent. The police department had inadvertently stumbled on a fresh approach to crime—a formula that is being adopted around the country under the rubric of community policing. Instead of waiting for crimes to occur, police are addressing problems that often attract crime: general disorder and decay.

Supporters of this new philosophy may not know it, but they are reviving a classic Christian understanding that crime is not only an individual act but also a violation of the social order. Hence, one of the best ways to fight crime is to restore order. For example, not long ago, New York City's Precinct 75 was one of the most dangerous places in America. Then the NYPD decided to show zero tolerance for any violation of public order. Officers stopped all traffic violators (which often led to finding drugs and guns). They chased away loiterers (who often turned out to be drug dealers looking for a sale). In three years, homicides dropped from 126 to 47.

After a gunfight in a Baltimore housing project, police worked with local agencies to upgrade street lighting, trim shrubbery, clean alleys, build a playground. Burglaries were reduced 80 percent, auto larceny 100 percent.

These success stories illustrated what criminologist James Q. Wilson calls the broken-window theory. Sociologists have discovered that if a window in a building is broken and left unrepaired, in a short time all the windows will be broken. Why? Because a smashed window sends a message that no one cares, that further vandalism will incur no penalty. And once a neighborhood tolerates minor violations like window-breaking, soon serious crime follows. A small breakdown of order—slothful maintenance—leads to major chaos.

The job of the police used to include fixing broken windows—that is, maintaining public order. According to Eric Monkkonen in *Police in Urban America: 1860-1920*, police developed the first food and soup lines. They built police stations with extra space where migrants could stay until they found work. They referred beggars to charitable agencies. And yes, they helped lost children find their way home.

But beginning in the early twentieth century, the role of the police was increasingly restricted: they were only to combat crime. They were to wait until called on the telephone. The final blow fell when the Supreme Court struck down an antivagrancy statute in 1972 and a statute against loitering in 1983. A domino effect followed as lower courts overturned state and municipal laws designed to restrain behavior in public places. Many major cities stood by helplessly as streets, parks, and subways succumbed to antisocial behavior, such as scribbling of graffiti and panhandling. These were soon followed by outright criminal behavior, such as assault and robbery.

## The Key to Restoring a Stable Culture

To reverse the destruction of our culture, we need to revive the classic Christian understanding of order. The biblical word *shalom* does not mean merely the absence of conflict: it means the establishment of right relationships—of justice and harmony. As Augustine wrote, true peace does not mean merely eliminating violence, it means establishing a just order—the "tranquility of order."

This principle holds in virtually any social situation. When I visit prisons, I witness a vivid difference in institutions that demand order: where floors are shiny and bunks are neat, morale is noticeably higher, discipline problems diminish. Schools experience the same effect when they maintain dress and behavior codes. When a neighborhood enforces high standards of order, it can effectively discourage crime within its borders. To cite another great Christian authority, William Wilberforce noted that "the most efficient way to prevent the greater crimes is by punishing the smaller, and by endeavoring to repress the general spirit of licentiousness, which is the parent of every kind of vice."

Fortunately, we don't have to wait for our local police forces to catch on. A few years ago in Montgomery, Alabama, fifty

Christian teenagers descended on a neighborhood determined to tackle a common allurement to crime: overgrown bushes that provide hiding places for vandals, burglars, and muggers. Armed with hedge clippers and weed whackers, the teens trimmed towering hedges and thinned low-hanging tree branches. They even replaced burned-out lights and installed peepholes in doors.

The project was called Youth Cutting Down on Crime, and it was organized by the Montgomery chapter of Neighbors Who Care, a Prison Fellowship ministry that mobilized churches to provide practical assistance to crime victims.

Like most other Americans, Christians are concerned about the alarming decline of morality, spirituality, and societal order in our culture. But unlike other Americans, we have a philosophy that gives us a larger answer than merely arresting more people and building bigger prisons. An effective strategy must start by asking fundamental philosophical questions: What makes a "good" community? What is the right order of society?

Investing time and money in building a rightly ordered society is the most powerful antidote to chaos and cultural decline. More important, it is a powerful witness to the biblical ideal of *shalom* in a decaying world.

When it comes to stopping the cultural decline of our young people, you can start by not demonstrating slothfulness on your own part. Your example will give a sense of order to your children's lives. Keep your house and yard clean and demand that your children clean up their rooms. Don't let them go out in public in clothes that are too revealing or sloppy. Take care to monitor what your kids watch on TV; you may end up tossing the TV into the trash. Extreme, yes, but better than giving the merchants of cool a free run at our kids.

Second, insist on family time. I know one family, devout Christians, who have meals together no matter what teenage activity is sacrificed. Third, keep hammering away at those who market tawdry values to our kids. Networks and advertisers do respond when enough people voice their outrage at objectionable programming. Remember what happened after Columbine? The WB TV network immediately yanked—temporarily, at least—an episode of a show that involved school violence.

When it comes to the broader culture, Christians need to be conscious of the subtle ways in which our nation is sinking into sloth. We must resist the slide by creating strong countercultural influences. We can start by elevating our own standards in speech and dress. We can uphold our absolute standard for morality in spite of what others do around us. One good place to start is in our worship services. I realize that casual is "in" for contemporary services—but "casual" should be decorous. We also should cultivate higher tastes. Christian art and music should not mimic the styles of their degraded secular counterparts.

The apostle Paul could not have imagined, sitting in a Roman jail cell, how appropriate his words to the church in Philippi would be for Christians 2,000 years later: "Whatever is true, whatever is noble, whatever is right, whatever is pure, whatever is lovely, whatever is admirable—if anything is excellent or praise-worthy—think about such things" (Philippians 4:8). Nothing less than thinking about such things and acting upon them can rescue our culture from following the fate Jeremiah prophesied for ancient Israel and the fate Solzhenitsyn prophesied for America.

# 6

## REBUILDING THE COMMUNITY OF TRUTH

# 6

## REBUILDING THE
## COMMUNITY OF TRUTH

It was the dream of a lifetime for George O'Leary: a chance to coach the world's most prestigious football team—Notre Dame's Fighting Irish.[1] But the dream soon became a nightmare. The day after he signed his contract with Notre Dame, O'Leary's résumé was sent to the press—a résumé that included "inaccuracies" about his education and college football letters. A few days later, O'Leary resigned in disgrace, the victim of his own long-ago lies.

It's an example of what's become an epidemic of lying.

In recent years, politicians and pundits, professors and even Pulitzer Prize winners have been caught dealing in deceit. One of the nation's most respected historians, Stephen Ambrose, plagiarized portions of other historians' works and—notwithstanding his public apology—seemed hardly disturbed by the resulting controversy.

Historian Joseph Ellis, who won the Pulitzer Prize for his book, *Founding Brothers*, was caught inventing a Vietnam War record for himself. So was Tim Johnson, manager of the Toronto Blue Jays. Gloria Steinem's claim about the number of women who die of eating disorders—supposedly 150,000 a year—turned out to be a huge feminist hoax. James Patterson and Peter Kim, authors of *The Day America Told the Truth*, estimate that 91 percent of us regularly embroider the truth. "We lie and don't even think about it," Patterson and Kim write.

Why has lying become so much more prevalent? Some scholars believe the problem arose out of the gradual adoption of a utilitarian ethic—one that began eroding the traditional Christian ethic in the West in the middle to late nineteenth century. This ethic says the (good) end justifies the means—that if a lie helps more than harms, then we should feel free to employ one.

In the late twentieth century, the rise of postmodern deconstructionism on college campuses exacerbated this problem. Postmodernists teach that the truth is not merely irrelevant; they believe it simply doesn't exist. As Lynne Cheney observes in her book, *Telling the Truth*, academics "leaped beyond the commonsense observation that people's descriptions of reality differ to the conclusion that there is no independent reality and thus no basis for making judgments about truth—or falsity." For these academics, truth claims are "the constructs of dominant groups—the creations of the powerful," Cheney writes. "Might makes right, in other words; and so intimidation was a perfectly natural way to try to gain assent."

The assault on truth has spread beyond academia to infect the arts, law, journalism, and psychotherapy—and Cheney points out that the grim results have been occurring for decades. For instance, way back in 1988, when it turned out that New York teenager Tawana Brawley had lied about being sexually assaulted by white men, *The Nation* claimed that "it doesn't matter whether the crime occurred or not" because it symbolizes "what actually happens to too many black women."

Most people reflexively assume that scientists with their stated commitment to the pursuit of accurate conclusions based on factual data and hard evidence, hold to a rigid standard of truth. Evolution, at least, which they assert to be a fact, has been empirically proven, right?

Wrong. Sure, there's evidence that evolution takes place *within* a species—but the fossil record has not yielded evidence of one species becoming another, as Darwin confidently predicted. This lack of evidence has not gone unnoticed by sociologist Rodney Stark. Stark calls himself neither an evolutionist nor an advocate of Intelligent Design; instead, he says, he is merely a scholar pursuing the evidence where it leads. In *For the Glory of God*, Stark offers startling evidence that Darwinists have covered up mounting flaws in their theory. He concludes that the battle over evolution is hardly a case of "heroic" scientists fighting off the persecution of religious fanatics. Instead, from the start, evolution "has primarily been an attack on religion by militant atheists who wrap themselves in the mantle of science in an effort to refute all religious claims concerning a creator—an effort that has also often attempted to suppress all scientific criticisms of Darwin's work."

Committed Darwinists continue this strategy today. For example, when biochemist Michael Behe published *Darwin's Black Box*, he argued that complex structures like proteins cannot be assembled piecemeal, with gradual improvement of function. Instead, like a mousetrap, all the parts—catch, spring, hammer, and so forth—must be assembled simultaneously, or the protein doesn't work.

Behe's thesis faced a challenge from the nation's leading expert on cell structure, Dr. Russell Doolittle at the University of California San Diego. Doolittle cited a study on bloodletting in the journal *Cell* that supposedly disproved Behe's argument. Behe immediately read the article—and realized that the study proved just the opposite: it supported his theory. Behe confronted Doolittle, who privately acknowledged that he was wrong—but declined to make a public retraction.

So who's really squelching truth? Those who invite us to follow the evidence wherever it leads—or those demanding that we ignore it? The folks who want both evolution and Intelligent Design taught in school, with all their strengths and weaknesses—or those who attempt to silence any opposition?

Those who maintain that truth exists, and that telling falsehoods is wrong, are increasingly under assault. "Fact fetishists" is how New York University professor Thomas Bender characterizes people who insist on accuracy. When reporters hounded him about Clintonian lies, then-White House aide George Stephanopoulos accused them of "an excess of literalism."

Postmodernism has filtered down to the masses; today, even the man on the street sees little wrong with lying. While *Washington Post* sportswriter Tony Kornheiser agreed that a religious college like Notre Dame was "completely right in separating itself from George O'Leary," he argued that "some people" will suggest that O'Leary's lies are "insignificant" when compared to his twenty-year coaching record.

In the pages of the *New York Post*, that's exactly what a sports fan did suggest. "I think Notre Dame is acting holier than thou," huffed salesman Jim McNulty; O'Leary should be judged not on his integrity, but on his coaching record. It's the perfect postmodern answer to lying: it's perfectly acceptable to reinvent ourselves, because what we say and do matter less than how people perceive us.

## Truth or Consequences

Worldviews do matter. The dominant attitude of recent decades says there are no moral truths—that we should simply live for the moment and get whatever we can out of life. This worldview has led to the crisis in truth we are experiencing. We are ignoring moral restraints that would hold us to truth, even labeling them intolerant.

C. S. Lewis showed us why a high concept of absolute truth is imperative and the disastrous results that can follow when that concept is lost. His book, *Miracles*, was prophetic, penned before most Christians were aware of the emerging philosophy of naturalism, the belief that there is a naturalistic explanation for everything in the universe. Lewis demonstrated that naturalism is self-destructing: if nature is all there is, then life is nothing but a cosmic accident. Even our minds—and thoughts—are nothing but "accidental by-product of the movement of atoms."[2]

But if all thoughts are the result of atoms knocking about in our brains, there is no reason to regard them as trustworthy or true—including the thoughts of the naturalist. Thus naturalism leads to the conclusion that the philosophy itself is not true.

It also undercuts any objective morality, opening a door to

tyranny. In *The Abolition of Man*, Lewis warned that naturalism turns human beings into objects to be controlled and turns values into "mere natural phenomena"—which can be selected and inculcated into a passive population by powerful Conditioners. He predicted a time when those who want to remold human nature "will be armed with the powers of an omnicompetent state and an irresistible scientific technique."[3] Thus "man's conquest of nature" in reality means "the rule of the Conditioners over the conditioned human material."[4]

This prediction was fleshed out in *That Hideous Strength*, a portentous allegory about an institution called N.I.C.E., formed to carry out an ambitious utopian vision to "improve" humanity (by coercion if necessary). The theme is that the loss of an objective morality paves the way to despotism, for then there is no control over the rulers beyond their own impulses. In Lewis's words, "The very idea of freedom presupposes some objective moral law which overarches rulers and ruled alike."[5]

Clearly the loss of the concept of absolute truth has consequences that reach far beyond the perceived "harmlessness" of inventing self-promoting bogus histories and manipulating data.

## TRUTH AND THE CHURCH

The philosophy that underlies the current fluid concept of truth and the tolerance of lying has spread even into the Christian community. Nowhere is it more apparent than in the movement known as the "emerging" church. This moment's leaders mean well: their aim is to communicate Christianity to a generation that has bought into the postmodern way of thinking. But I fear that in their efforts toward accommodation, they come perilously near capitulation.

Distressed about my widely circulated exchanges with an "emerging church" leader, a young theologian confronted me after a conference. He urged me to try to understand them. "You might be surprised by how much you agree on," he said.

Maybe I had been too harsh. After all, the theologian—we'll call him Jim—argued that emerging church leaders are trying to translate the gospel for a postmodern generation. That's a commendable goal, I agreed. Though in their effort to reach postmoderns—who question the existence and knowability of truth—I expressed fear that they are coming dangerously close to teaching that objective truth does not exist.

A lengthy e-mail exchange with Jim followed. In defense of emerging church leaders, he insisted that truth is paradoxical, simultaneously personal and propositional. It is objectively true that Jesus Christ is Lord no matter what anyone thinks, Jim wrote. But, he added, "Propositional truth is not the highest truth. Indeed, the highest truth is personal."

Like all statements that can lead us into error, those have the ring of truth. Of course, truth becomes relational when we come to Jesus, Truth himself. But our doing that isn't what makes it true. He is the truth whether or not we ever experience him. Scripture is never less than revealed propositional truth.

Jim argued that one prominent emerging church leader won't say this for fear that the greater points he's trying to make won't be heard. Okay, I conceded, his motives may be good, but his position can lead people to think that truth depends on experience or comprehension.

Jim continued to plead for my understanding. Emerging church leaders are only seeking to challenge the church to go beyond static orthodoxy. Good, I replied—but what's new? I've been trying to get people out of pews to live their faith in prisons for thirty years.

Fearful that I was being influenced by stereotypes, I asked my associate Anne Morse to visit a leading emerging church. The service was a bit unsettling to a traditionalist, she reported, with no Bibles or hymnals in sight. During the service, congregants were free to engage in activities at various "stations" of the building: praying, journaling, or tithing. The pastor, who lacks formal seminary training, offered not a sermon, but the story of his decision to "follow Jesus."

But style is not really the issue. I've worshiped all over the world, in former prison torture chambers, under jungle overgrowth in Sri Lanka, and in homes of persecuted believers. And I recognize that the emerging church is trying to engage the postmodern mindset as Paul did at Mars Hill, picking up on Athenian cultural artifacts. Once he did that, however, Paul also taught them why they were wrong. He didn't sanctify the altar to the unknown god or say that pagans have things to teach us, as at least one emerging church leader does (when, for example, he says Buddhists have things to teach Christians about meditation).

The e-mails kept coming back to that one stubborn question: what is truth? My experience is that most mainstream evangelicals are so steeped in the experiential gospel that they never think about truth propositionally. A Barna Group survey in 2009 found that only "one-third of all adults (34%) believe that moral truth is absolute and unaffected by circumstances.

Slightly less than half of the born-again adults (46%) believe in absolute moral truth."[6]

The arguments of some emerging church leaders, I fear, draw us perilously close to the trap set by postmodern deconstructionist Stanley Fish. Fish claimed that postmodernists don't really deny the existence of truth. He said there is simply no "independent standard of objectivity." So truth can't be proved to others; therefore, it can't be known—a verbal sleight of hand.

For evangelicalism (let alone emerging churches) to buy into that would undermine the very foundation of our faith. Theologian Donald A. Carson puts his finger precisely on the epistemological problem: of course, truth is relational, Carson writes. But before it can be relational, it has to be understood as objective. Truth is truth. It is, in short, ultimate reality. Fortunately, Jim came to see this.

The emerging church can offer a healthy corrective if it encourages us to more winsomely draw postmodern seekers to Christ wherever we find them—including coffee houses and pubs. And yes, worship styles need to be more inviting, and the strength of relationship and community experienced. But these must not deter us from making a solid apologetic defense of the knowability of truth.

If we could be assured that questionable approaches to absolute truth were limited to one isolated movement within Christendom, the problem would not seem threatening. But that is not the case. It has become clear that alien philosophies undermining truth have infiltrated virtually all Christian churches. For example, I received a letter recently from Julie, a Bible-study leader in a solid evangelical church, who wrote to tell me of a discussion with moms in her church about their favorite books for children. She was appalled that so many touted books with naturalistic themes.

Julie picked up one of the books—a Berenstein Bears title— and showed the moms the page that read, "Nature is all there is, ever was, or ever will be." They didn't get it. The moms were too young to remember Carl Sagan or the famous line from his book and film, *Cosmos*: "The cosmos is all there is, all there ever was, and all there ever will be." "How do we wake people up?" Julie asked in her letter.

Good question. If the polls are correct, false ideas have penetrated not only children's books but also our most basic beliefs. Gallup reports that 20 percent of born-again Christians believe in reincarnation and 26 percent in astrology. Forty-five percent of those that the Barna Group classifies as born-again believe that "if people are good enough they can earn a place in heaven." And Wade Clark Roof in *Spiritual Marketplace* writes that half of born-again baby boomers believe all religions are "equally good and true," almost half have no involvement in a conservative Protestant church, and a quarter believe in communicating with the dead!

Admittedly, poll data can be ambiguous, and the term *born-again* has certainly been trivialized. Still, the data paint a shocking picture of the state of evangelical Christianity. On any Sunday, an alarming number who fill our pews are either biblically illiterate or, worse, syncretists.

How can we explain this? Roof offers one answer: boomers tend to substitute feelings for objective reality, seeking self-centered spirituality over the structured demands of organized religion. With self-fulfillment their standard, they pick and choose, as if at a salad bar, from any belief system that provides comfort or meaning.

Has relativism so invaded the church that adults have lost the capacity to disciple their own youth? In my darkest moments, I couldn't have imagined it. But a recent episode makes me wonder.

A graduate of Prison Fellowship's Centurion program (an intensive course in biblical worldview) sponsors a voluntary Christian club at her local middle school. Forty-three students eagerly signed up for the thirteen-week course. Everything went well until the students reached lesson 10, which led them through a series of choices to learn the difference between matters of taste and truth. One of the choices, "believing Islam, Buddhism, or Christianity" flashed on the screen.

Our Centurion—I'll call her Joanne—told me "the students went nuts." She was shocked when seven of the eight small-group leaders, supposedly mature Christians, balked at distinguishing Christianity as true and other religions as false.

Joanne urged them to talk to their parents or pastors, believing these authority figures would straighten them out. The next day, they came back with their answers—and they were appalling. One teen's pastor said that no one can be sure of truth, that "it's all perspective." Parents of the seven leaders agreed that their teens shouldn't say that Christianity alone is true, because that could offend others. One girl had written a paper on "Why We Shouldn't Hurt Others' Feelings by Claiming Our Way Is Right." Joanne was forced to shelve chapter 10. "They can't teach what they don't believe," she said.

The spirit of the age shuns absolutes, and this has weakened the church's capacity to raise such challenges even if we were disposed to. A seminary dean told me his students all say they believe in absolute truth, but at the same time are reluctant to "impose" their views. Serious laity are even less inclined to challenge one another in today's relativistic environment, for fear of being thought of as intolerant or bigoted. Mark Dever, pastor of Washington's Capitol Hill Baptist Church, sums up the problem bluntly: "The church has lost the capacity to judge between good and evil, truth and falsehood."

## REAFFIRMING THE TRUTH

How did America and its churches lose the concept of truth so firmly held by the general populace only two short generations ago? According to sociologist Robert Bellah, it's because we have lost what he calls our "community of memory."

In the 1980s, Bellah conducted interviews with two hundred average, middle-class Americans, searching for what, borrowing from Alexis de Tocqueville, he called the "habits of the heart" that guide us. Many respondents reported no sense of community or social obligation of any kind. They saw the world as a fragmented place of choice and freedom that yielded little meaning or comfort.

Bellah called this phenomenon "ontological individualism"— the belief that the individual is the only source of meaning. It stands in stark contrast to what he called "biblical" and "republican" traditions, which provide a reference point of meaning outside the individual—telling us about the nature of the world, society, and ourselves. These traditions are embodied in "communities of memory" such as religious groups, traditional families, and cultural associations. They communicate a sense of order and context from one generation to the next. Bellah predicted that such pervasive individualism could destroy the subtle ties that bind people together and threaten the very stability of our social order.

Tragically, Bellah may have been prophetic. We have already seen what relativism and radical individualism have done to the family, which is so essential for the transmission of manners and morals from one generation to the next. I've seen the consequences of this in two generations of prison inmates. When I walk through the nation's cellblocks, I speak to kids about God the Father. They look at me as if I'd said a dirty word. Most don't know who their father is. They're like feral children, devoid of any kind of moral instruction.

If you lose the community of memory for one generation, you can make it up. But after two generations, you've severed the arteries of civilization that transmit truth and virtue. Clearly, the stakes are enormous, not just for the church but also for our culture.

If there's one place the community of memory must be maintained—even as the family and other cultural institutions falter—it is the church. We, after all, are people who live by revealed truth. The apostles' teaching was handed down from one generation to the next, faithfully transmitted with meticulous care. During the Dark Ages, Irish monks copied and preserved the Bible and other books. They understood that civilization could not survive if one did not pass down the wisdom of previous generations.

If we hope to preserve the concept of truth in the general culture, we as a church must preserve the ability to know the truth ourselves.

The good news is that while America's tolerance of lying is greater than ever, Americans retain enough of their Judeo-Christian ethic that they are still scandalized when a public figure lies. We have to help our neighbors understand what's behind the current propensity for lying: a worldview that denies the existence of truth itself, which merely exacerbates our human fallenness in this area. And then we must point them to the Author of truth, the one who said, "I am the Way, the Truth, and the Life."

Pastors I've consulted agree that there is a problem, and they believe the answer is in better expository preaching. That is needed, but I question whether this alone will turn the tide. To teach believers to be discerning demands a systemic effort to examine how Christianity stacks up against other claims in every area of life. When worldviews are honestly compared, the truth of Christianity (and the untruth of other views) becomes clear.

It is vital that Christians become more discriminating. Discerning Christians would have clearly seen the pagan presuppositions behind that statement in the Berenstein Bears book that so many moms unthinkingly embraced. As Julie discovered, believers may understand Scripture but still not recognize naturalistic claims that undermine biblical belief.

Most importantly, when we discern what is false we must have the courage to label it as such. Some seekers might be driven away, but better that than the insidious spread of syncretism within the church.

The church today needs to take a lesson from one of the heroic figures of a century ago. Alarmed by the rise of modernism and false teachings spreading even in evangelical churches, New Testament scholar J. Gresham Machen published a scathing attack in his classic, *Christianity and Liberalism*. Machen argued that the beliefs many were embracing weren't simply a new version of Christianity; rather, they constituted another religion altogether. The book was a sobering jolt to many Christians.

So too we should label today's syncretism another religion. Much of what passes for born-again Christianity may suit the spirit of the age, but it isn't authentic Christianity. As historian Paul Johnson notes, Christianity is a historical religion that deals in facts and events. Among those facts is that Jesus, the Son of God, was born of a virgin, in a specific time and place. Johnson cites the mounting archaeological discoveries that have almost universally supported the biblical accounts. And the life of Jesus, he notes, is better authenticated than most other figures of antiquity, like Aristotle and Julius Caesar. As Johnson puts it, "It is not now the men of faith; it is the skeptics who have reason to fear the course of discovery." This truth needs to be communicated both to those in the pews and those in our pulpits as well.

# 7

# CRACKING THE ETHICS CODE IN SCIENCE

# 7

# CRACKING THE
# ETHICS CODE IN SCIENCE

In a Senate hearing room, the late Christopher Reeve was testifying in support of embryonic stem-cell research.[1] Sitting in his wheelchair, breathing with a ventilator, the former star of *Superman* films made a sympathetic figure. And then someone raised an uncomfortable question: is it ethical to take a life to save a life? Embryonic stem-cell research does, after all, destroy human embryos.

Reeve countered: "I thought it was the job of the government to do the greatest good for the greatest number." Senators and reporters nodded in agreement. Obviously, they didn't get it. If the government really embraced "the greatest good for the greatest number," Reeve himself might be dead. After all, Reeve's therapies, his doctors, his aides, and his motorized wheelchair cost millions—money that could, instead, fund basic medical care for hundreds of poor children.

Of course, Reeve could afford to pay for all of this himself— a fortunate fact should the government have taken his "greatest good" advice. But he continued to ask taxpayers to spend millions on research to treat spinal cord injuries. Given that vastly more Americans need immunizations than a cure for paralysis, wouldn't a "greatest good" policy mean spending scarce research funds on immunizations instead of paralysis research?

I've used this vignette, which I mentioned in chapter 1 as well, in speeches, and to my shock, I've found that even Christians nod in agreement with Reeve's reasoning—until I explain just where this thinking leads. Have we all unthinkingly become practical utilitarians?

Reeve was echoing the arguments of Princeton philosopher Peter Singer, the quintessential moral utilitarian. Singer believes morality cannot be judged by any transcendent standard. Instead, he suggests we ask whether a particular action will increase the world's sum total of happiness.

For example, Singer believes parents should, instead of spending money on lifesaving surgery for their child, send the money to save a hundred African children from starvation; doing so would increase the world's total amount of happiness. Singer scorns traditional teachings about the sanctity of human life, believing that some people—encephalitic babies, for example—are not actually "persons." He argues that parents should be allowed to kill their handicapped newborns (a healthy replacement baby would live a happier life), and favors euthanasia for sick and elderly people who have lost the basic capacity for mental functioning and who create a burden on others.

This is the "greatest good" philosophy that Christopher Reeve espoused. I wonder if he knew that Singer, on his first day at Princeton, was greeted by protesters from Not Dead Yet, a group of people who—like Reeve—were wheelchair-bound. Unlike Reeve, they understood exactly where Singer's teaching leads: euthanasia for those considered burdens on society.

The ethical approach to the application of research promoted by Reeve and Singer illustrates the ever-increasing influence Charles Darwin's evolutionary theory holds over science and medicine. When we look beneath the high-sounding logic and rationale of many life and death decisions, "survival of the fittest" is fast becoming the new standard for determination. In brightly lit hospital operating rooms, crowded nursing homes, busy research labs, and doctors' offices, an unannounced, lethal war is being waged against the weakest of the weak: handicapped infants, the elderly, and humans at the embryonic stage of life.

The opening shot in this war was fired when the modern eugenics movement came into fashion some eighty years ago. The first targets were the "feebleminded" and people of the "wrong" race. Leading scientists in the early decades of the twentieth century, enamored with Darwin's theories, became eugenics advocates. Historian Richard Weikart, in *From Darwin to Hitler: Evolutionary Ethics, Eugenics, and Racism in Germany*, writes that while Darwin wasn't the first to argue that the strong and healthy have higher value than the weak and sick, or that some races are inferior, he provided a scientific foundation for those beliefs.

Some scientists actually compared the mentally ill to apes. Textbooks reported allegedly scientific findings that Africans, Native Americans, and Australian aborigines were subhuman. The eugenics movement brought about the sterilization of thousands of supposedly "inferior" people.

Even the U.S. Supreme Court weighed in. Among the most enthusiastic proponents of forced sterilization was Supreme Court Justice Oliver Wendell Holmes, who wrote in *Buck v. Bell* (1927) that "it is better for all the world" if "society can prevent those who are manifestly unfit from continuing their kind. . . . Three generations of imbeciles are enough." The result was often tragic. Included in Holmes's third generation of "imbeciles" was a girl named Vivian Buck, who was no such thing—nor was her mother, who was sterilized after Vivian's birth. As Harry Bruinius documents in *Better for All the World*, determinations of "feeblemindedness" and "imbecility" were based on little more than pseudoscience and prejudice.

This pseudoscience was all the rage in Vienna and Munich, where a young Adolf Hitler proposed his radical ideas for the "master race." Weikart writes that among the few authors we know Hitler admired, some were steeped in that culture. The ultimate result of those theories were the long lines leading to gas chambers—the mass murder of Jews, Gypsies, homosexuals, and the developmentally disabled.

Seventy years later, eugenic ideas are surfacing again, masquerading as humanitarian progress—as in research labs where scientists destroy "leftover" human embryos to find cures for diseases, or in sperm banks where women select their baby's father from hundreds of donors on the basis of intelligence or gifts, or in doctors' offices where parents feel subtle pressure to abort imperfect fetuses, or in hospitals when futile-care policies allow doctors to decide who lives and who dies. Today, some ethicists, like Singer, brazenly argue that it's permissible to kill disabled children after they're born—children like my autistic grandson, Max—all in the seductive guise of maximizing human happiness.

This utilitarian logic is being applied not only to taking life but also to creating it in the image of man. English scientists are attempting to create "designer babies" by transplanting the nucleus from the cell of a woman with defective mitochondria into the healthy egg of another woman. The resulting child would have three genetic parents. It's the first step toward genetic engineering of human beings.

Eugenics, once discredited, has made a lethal comeback. Today, scientists are fashioning a "master race" not by herding "inferior" people into gas chambers, but by practicing involuntary euthanasia throughout the life cycle. As Judeo-Christian influence erodes in Western society, traditional ethical norms are giving way to the only remaining absolute: maximizing happiness. But sacrificing one to benefit all soon makes all vulnerable. If we follow the deadly logic of modern utilitarianism, other questions will soon confront us: Why not take the body parts of prisoners—dead and alive—to save others? Why feed those unable to work or provide medical care to someone in the last stages of illness?

Evolutionary ethics give us no reason to eschew moral horrors. Indeed, as Weikart points out, the early Darwinists stated quite boldly that mass death was necessary to improve the race. They "claimed that the winners in the struggle for existence have to 'stride over the corpses of the vanquished,'" Weikart notes. "This is what they saw as natural law. Natural evil serves a good purpose then, that is, of producing higher species."

## THE LOGICAL RESULT OF DARWINIAN ETHICS

As we noted in chapter 6, Oxford's C. S. Lewis saw it all coming more than fifty years ago: scientists and politicians debating human cloning, gene manipulation, controlling our progeny—all in the name of humanity, of course. "If any one age really attains, by eugenics and scientific education, the power to make its descendants what it pleases," Lewis prophetically warned, "all men who live after are the patients of that power."[2] They will be slaves to the "dead hand of the great planners and Conditioners."[3]

This is ultimately the issue facing us in today's intense debates over embryonic stem-cell research, so-called therapeutic cloning, and the like. Beyond the questions argued in Congress—whether embryos are humans or merely, as the *New York Times* puts it, "a ball of cells"—lurks the largely ignored question Lewis posed: what becomes of humanity if we become the controllers?

The biotech revolution has surged forward as the defining issue of this new century. On the one hand, it holds out great promise for medical advances enhancing life and health for all humankind. On the other, it raises unprecedented ethical issues.

Christians are not Luddites; we simply insist that science remain tethered to moral truth. But the biotech revolution is moving like a steamroller, fueled by huge potential profits, crushing everything—including moral restraint—in its path. Secular ethics, in this relativistic age, have been drained of moral content; they can be based only on utilitarianism (doing the greatest good for the greatest number) or pragmatism (doing whatever works). Thus Singer advocates infanticide for defective babies and Dutch-style euthanasia of the most infirm elderly.

Admittedly, in the political debate, the utilitarians apparently have seized the moral high ground with powerful humanitarian appeals. They offer dazzling predictions that embryonic stem-cell research will lead to cures for Parkinson's, Alzheimer's, and other diseases. Not incidentally, they appeal to self-interest as well. Who doesn't have a relative so afflicted (and who doesn't fear such affliction for oneself)? Unused embryos are going to be destroyed anyway, they argue—so using them to help the desperately sick is the truly "pro-life" position.

Some sixty-five years ago, German doctors made similar arguments, justifying the killing of the physically and mentally retarded, whom they described as *lebensunwertes Leben* —"life unworthy of life."

The proposals of Singer and Reeve violate ethical norms upheld by Christians and held dear by the vast majority of humanity since the beginning of time. But what many do not see is that their philosophy also leads to absurdity. Rejecting the uniqueness of human life, Singer claims that drawing distinctions between humans and animals is "speciesism." So—quite logically—he professes to find nothing morally objectionable about bestiality (sex with animals), a view that shocks even non-Christians. (When my colleague, ethicist Nigel M. de S. Cameron, pressed Singer in a debate on the question of the animal's consent, it put Singer on the defensive.)

In utilitarianism, we encounter a philosophy dramatically at odds with Christianity. The Scriptures teach that God created humans in his own image, giving each a unique moral character. Christianity, as Mother Teresa used to say, is anti-statistical. Every human, at every stage in life, has intrinsic, not merely instrumental, worth. This means it's never right to create and then kill one person to find a cure for another. Of course, we all want to see loved ones relieved of their suffering. But it shows what we're up against when even many Christians fail to grasp the implications of practical utilitarianism.

In one sense, we can be grateful for Singer. He does what Francis Schaeffer urged us to make secularists do—that is, take their reasonable-sounding philosophies and carry them to their logical and often preposterous conclusions. I've discovered that this tactic is the best way to penetrate the postmodern fog. If biblical revelation is true, any proposition that is inconsistent with it can be shown to be irrational.

Life-and-death issues like embryonic stem-cell research won't go away. If we don't make the case against utilitarianism, policies that today make most of us recoil may one day, as our moral sensibilities become anesthetized, elicit nothing more than a shrug. And then, as the philosophy of "the greatest good for the greatest number" takes hold, the Christopher Reeves of the world will be in peril—and so will the rest of us.

## CHALLENGING UTILITARIAN ETHICS

If we expect to restore sanity and true ethics to science and medicine, we need to challenge the premises of the utilitarians' case. For example, predictions of what cloning and embryonic stem-cell research may accomplish have been grossly overstated, and experiments have led to some grotesque results. Nor have proponents established that only embryonic stem cells can meet the research needs; promising results have been achieved from easily harvested placental and adult stem cells—the use of which presents no ethical dilemmas.

And what about those "leftover" embryos that are just going to be destroyed? Couples who have adopted them ought to show off their beautiful "post embryos," now healthy children.

We should point out that many of the scientists involved in embryonic stem-cell research (and the so-called ethicists hired by biotech industries) are poised to make huge profits from their deadly studies. This goes largely unreported.

Life at every stage is precious in God's design. We must help our neighbors understand that this aspect of the Christian worldview—the conviction that all life is sacred—provides the only defense for the weakest in our midst. If, as I believe, the character of a society is ultimately judged by how well it cares for the poor and the weak, what does the return of eugenics tell us about our nation?

But our greatest service as Christians is to do what we best do, that is, raise transcendent moral arguments. To sacrifice one person for the good of many can never be justified. Evil often masquerades as good; the worst atrocities are performed in the name of humanitarian causes. And we must press the logic of the utilitarian argument to its ultimate conclusion: sacrificing one to benefit all soon makes all vulnerable.

Christians must do more than assert the truth that life begins at conception; people dismiss that as arbitrary and outdated dogma. We must also raise the question Lewis did in *The Abolition of Man:* what does it really mean if we set ourselves up as the master of the future destiny of the human race?

Lewis answers: if man with his technology makes the

ultimate conquest over nature, he will soon find that nature has conquered him. "If man chooses to treat himself as raw material, raw material he will be,"[4] manipulated by dehumanized conditioners.

The twentieth century will be remembered for the triumph of liberal democracy over tyranny. What tragic irony if the twenty-first century, by exchanging transcendent moral truth for the cold calculus of utilitarianism, ushers in a new and even more terrifying form of tyranny.

I will close this chapter with a story, which should inspire those of us who tend to think today's ethical breakdown in science and medicine looms too large for any one person to confront.

As I found my seat in the ornate East Room of the White House, memories flared. I had been in this room hundreds of times during the years I served President Nixon. Today I was here for a much different reason: to hear President George W. Bush speak about human cloning.

I confess to having become somewhat jaded; America, I thought, had become so post-Christian that I would never again hear an American president explicitly embrace Christian teaching on a profound moral issue. President Bush proved me wrong, and in the process, I was given a remarkable example of God's sovereignty.

Standing at the podium, surrounded by people in wheelchairs, President Bush described the great advances in medicine—the cracking of the genetic code and potential victories over feared diseases. But then came a warning. "As we seek to improve human life," he said, "we must always preserve human dignity. Advances in medical technology must never come at the expense of human conscience. As we seek what is possible, we must also seek what is right, and we must not forget that even the most noble ends do not justify any means."

As I listened, my spine tingled—and not only from the president's inspiring words. Across the aisle I spotted ethicist Nigel Cameron, whom I had met twenty years before when he was a freshly minted Ph.D. running a study center in Scotland. We became friends, and I soon discovered his keen interest in bioethics.

At that time, few people even knew what the term meant, or thought about genetic engineering or cloning. For activists, abortion was the life issue. Over coffee one evening in Edinburgh, Nigel told me bioethics would emerge as the moral issue of the new millennium. He was so certain of this that he helped found the world's first bioethics journal, which began to awaken the Christian world. Nigel was like a sentry on the forward outpost, spotting the real enemy: the prospect of technology unleashed from moral restraints.

Eighteen months before the president's speech, Nigel had become dean of Prison Fellowship's worldview ministry, and immediately set out—working with Sen. Sam Brownback (R-Kan.), Rep. Dave Weldon (R-Fla.), and others—to build a broad-based coalition. Gazing around the East Room, I realized many guests were there through Nigel's efforts.

There must have been many times over the years that Nigel became frustrated, wondering if he was wasting his time discussing an issue that seemed remote to so many. But there he was that day listening to the most powerful man in the world articulating, in the manner of a moral theologian, the case he had long fought for.

My eye then fell on another guest: Joni Eareckson Tada. As a teenager, Joni dove into shallow waters in Chesapeake Bay, tragically breaking her neck. Doomed to a life of quadriplegia in a wheelchair, Joni might have been consumed with self-pity. Instead, Joni is one of the most cheerful people I've ever known.

When President Bush finished speaking, he stepped down from the podium, embraced Joni, and kissed her. At that moment, it struck me that one reason God may have allowed Joni's tragedy was this moment of witness—not only to the president, but also to the world. Joni is the Christian counterpoint to Christopher Reeve and other celebrities who make emotionally appealing but dangerously utilitarian arguments for human cloning. Joni opposes the taking of human life for medical research, even if it could lead to relief for her suffering. She understands that abortion, euthanasia, cloning, and embryonic stem-cell research are all related to one great question: what does it mean to be human?

That single hour in the White House provides a dramatic answer to two frequently asked questions. The first is the age-old challenge: how a loving God can allow such suffering. Certainly, there is sin and suffering in our fallen world—from our own making. But as Joni's life and witness prove, God redeems that suffering.

The second question is one I hear with increasing frequency in our post-Christian culture: what difference can one person make? The problems are so huge; we feel helpless, and so we do nothing.

That response is a cop-out. Nigel did not think that way, nor did Joni. They pressed on, confident that a sovereign God would use them, as indeed he has. They remind us that God sets each of us in a particular time and place for a precise purpose. We must strengthen our resolve, no matter the obstacles, to fulfill that purpose in a fallen world.

# 8

# RESISTING THE TYRANNY OF THE COURTS

# 8

# RESISTING THE
# TYRANNY OF THE COURTS

The marble pillars of the Supreme Court building rise impe-
riously across the street from the U.S. Capitol—as though
these two branches of government were staring each other down,
the better to keep the balance of power.[1]

But in the summer of 1997, the U.S. Supreme Court, as
well as some U.S. district courts and various state supreme
courts, began to tilt the balance precariously. In this chapter I
will address three court decisions rendered within the past two
decades that clearly demonstrate the courts' attempt to assume
more power than the Constitution grants. Of particular concern
is their assumption of power to determine on their own terms
the limits of religious freedom. These decisions, beginning in the
1990s, opened the floodgates for a number of laws, rulings, and
government actions that have adversely affected the free exercise
of religion in our nation. If the trend is not reversed, I believe the
future of religious freedom in America is in jeopardy.

## BOERNE V. FLORES

The first of these decisions was the 1997 Supreme Court ruling in the case of *Boerne v. Flores*. The case involved a church which sued the city of Boerne, Texas, for its refusal to allow the enlargement of its building to accommodate congregational growth. The city's refusal was based on the fact that the church building had been designated a historical landmark and must therefore be preserved in its original state. With its decision in this case, the Court tilted the balance dangerously, precipitating what may become the greatest constitutional crisis of our age.

The primary issue in *Boerne* was the "free exercise" clause of the First Amendment. For some thirty-five years, the Court had held that religious practice could be curtailed only if the state showed a "compelling state interest" (e.g., protection of public health or safety). But in *Employment Division v. Smith* (1990) the Court dropped the "compelling interest" test, demoting religion to the level of a personal preference. Congress responded with the Religious Freedom Restoration Act (RFRA), restoring the "compelling interest" test. And in *Boerne*, the Court retaliated, striking down RFRA.

This unprecedented tit-for-tat raised two fundamental issues. First, religious liberties once again became vulnerable. In the interim between *Smith* and RFRA, an Ohio fire marshal threatened to fine Christmas Eve worshipers for carrying sacramental candles, an Illinois county forbade Orthodox Jews to wear yarmulkes in courtrooms, and a Maryland ordinance instructed a Catholic hospital to train its interns to perform abortions. Under *Boerne*, such violations of religious liberty began anew. In Texas,

Catholic schoolboys were forbidden to display rosaries around their necks, and in Los Angeles an Orthodox Jewish congregation was ejected from a neighborhood in which it had met for two decades.

But *Boerne* also raised a profound constitutional question: who determines what the Constitution means? RFRA was based on the Fourteenth Amendment, which gives Congress the power to enact legislation enforcing constitutional rights—applying, interpreting, or modifying them. But the Court argued that RFRA did more than enforce rights, it expanded a right. Congress has no power "to decree the substance" of a constitutional right, the majority huffed; it is the judiciary's prerogative to define what the Constitution means.

But this was sheer bluster. Contrary to what most Americans think, the Constitution does not give the Supreme Court final say on constitutional questions. And the Founders resisted the idea. If we gave "judges the right to decide what laws are constitutional," Jefferson warned, they would become "despots."

It was in 1803, in *Marbury v. Madison*, that the Court assumed the power of judicial review. Even so, three presidents have resisted Court orders: Thomas Jefferson refused to execute the Alien Imposition Act; Jackson spurned a Court order in a banking case; Lincoln rejected the Dred Scott decision.

Lincoln even asked Congress to overrule the Court —which it did, passing a law that reversed Dred Scott (1862). Congress likewise overrode Court decisions dealing with child labor (1938), prohibiting Orthodox Jews in the Air Force from wearing yarmulkes (1986), and requiring the Amish to pay Social Security taxes (1988). The Court's claim to an exclusive right to interpret the Constitution has no basis in law or history.

Worse, it is an assault on the very notion of self-government. The classical ideal of liberty is a people governing themselves— writing their own laws and hence ruled by their own vision of a good social order. To quote from "We Hold These Truths," a statement signed by forty-two Christian leaders (including me) on July 4, 1997, "Our nation was constituted by the agreement that 'we, the people,' through the representative institutions of republican government, would deliberate and decide how we ought to order our life together."

In *Boerne*, the Court myopically defended its own turf at the expense of democratic principle. If there was ever an example of a people deciding together, it was RFRA. The act won widespread popular support, passing unanimously in the House and with only three dissenting votes in the Senate. But no matter. The Court simply swept aside the national consensus.

## DALE V. BOY SCOUTS OF AMERICA

In a stunning decision rendered in 1999, the New Jersey Supreme Court ruled against the Boy Scouts for dismissing a homosexual scoutmaster.

The case involved assistant scoutmaster James Dale, who was dismissed after a newspaper identified him as co-president of the Gay/Lesbian Alliance at Rutgers University. Dale sued, and in *Dale v. The Boy Scouts of America* the court ruled unanimously in his favor.

The decision should not be read merely as an attack on the

Scouts. What made it so pernicious was its reasoning. It effectively erased the distinction between private and public organizations—which could potentially affect all other private groups, with devastating consequences for nonprofits and Christian ministries across the nation. Earlier decisions in other states had affirmed the right of Boy Scouts to define its mission and membership requirements as a private organization. But this time the court ruled that the group is a "public accommodation," like a restaurant, hotel, or department store—and thus was subject to state antidiscrimination laws.

The Court's reasoning was that Scouting is so large and recruits so widely that it is not "selective" enough to qualify as a private group. (Never mind that Scouting programs are open only to boys, only to certain ages, and only to those willing to abide by the Scout Law.) Moreover, the court noted that some Scout units are supported by local government groups like fire departments and law-enforcement agencies.

By this reasoning, however, any large group that recruits widely and works closely with government agencies could be reclassified as a "public accommodation," which could include Christian ministries, hospitals, charities, colleges, even churches. For example, at Prison Fellowship we have a "close relationship" with the government in order to reach the people we serve: prisoners. And yes, we issue invitations to one and all. Does this make us a "public accommodation," giving the state a right to dictate who we can hire?

But the Court's reasoning gets worse. It bluntly rejected Scouting's moral stand against homosexuality, dismissing it as "little more than prejudice." In a concurring opinion, Justice

Alan Handler renounced the "stereotype" that "homosexuals are inherently immoral." In short, the court assumed a right to decide not only what is legal, but also what qualifies as moral and immoral.

This represents a startling departure from previous cases, like the U.S. Supreme Court's 1995 ruling against homosexual groups that wanted to march in Boston's St. Patrick's Day parade. There the Court held that the state may not "trespass on [a group's] message" by forcing it to include those whose beliefs are diametrically opposed to its own. But in *Dale*, the justices felt free to trample all over the Scouts' message.

Worst of all, the court essentially decided it may even tell a group what its message really is. The court argued that the Scout Oath, which includes the promise "to keep myself . . . morally straight," does not imply moral opposition to homosexuality— although the Scouts have traditionally understood it just that way. Justice Handler even insisted that accepting homosexuals is not contrary to "the Boy Scouts' adherence to 'traditional moral values.'" In short, the court assumed a right to interpret the meaning of the Scouts' mission statements in a manner completely contrary to the Scouts' own interpretation.

This set a chilling precedent. "The ultimate meaning and implementation of the Boy Scouts' creeds are not for the government to decide," wrote Mark Tooley of the Institute on Religion and Democracy. For if government can tell private groups what their own creeds "really" mean, what is to prevent it from telling Christian ministries and churches what their creeds "really" mean, even if contrary to the way those creeds have traditionally been interpreted?

In the summer of 2000, the U.S. Supreme Court reversed the decision of the New Jersey court and ruled in favor of BSA by a narrow 5-4 decision. The decision was accompanied by a strongly worded dissent from Justice John Paul Stevens, who said, "Every state law prohibiting discrimination is designed to replace prejudice with principle." He further asserted that the Boy Scouts' exclusion of gay members did not square with its founding principles. He noted that the Boy Scouts sought to prepare young people "to make ethical choices over their lifetime in achieving their full potential" and to be "morally straight" and "clean." As these terms were defined in the Scout Handbook, Justice Stevens said, "It is plain as the light of day that neither one of these principles—'morally straight' and 'clean'—says the slightest thing about homosexuality. Indeed, neither term in the Boy Scouts' Law and Oath expresses any position whatsoever on sexual matters."[2]

Justice Stevens and his three fellow dissenters were apparently using the same logic they applied in a previous case, *Romer v. Evans* (1996), when the Court decreed that Colorado voters' opposition to special civil rights for homosexuals was motivated by "bigotry." As in *Dale*, the justices failed to recognize the validity of moral concern about homosexuality, relegating it to mere prejudice.

The high court's narrow ruling favoring the Boy Scouts in *Dale v. BSA* did not save the Scouts from a subsequent negative ruling on a closely related issue. In *Boy Scouts of America v. Wyman*, Connecticut State Comptroller Nancy Wyman excluded the Boy Scouts from the Connecticut State Employee Campaign, a charitable program in which the Scouts had participated for thirty years. The reason for her exclusion was that the Boy Scouts violated Connecticut's antidiscrimination laws by excluding homosexuals from participation in the leadership of the organization. The Scouts lost the case both in court and on appeal, and in the spring of 2004, the U.S. Supreme Court refused to revisit the ruling.[3]

## A.U.S.C. v. PRISON FELLOWSHIP MINISTRIES

According to one critic, the belief held by evangelicals and Prison Fellowship (PF) in the "substitutionary and atoning death of Jesus," reflects "a legalistic understanding of the sacrifice of Jesus, [which] is not shared by many Christians." So much for the central tenet of every historic creed and confession of the Christian church.

Where was this critique—in the *New York Times*? No, it was the finding of U.S. District Judge Robert Pratt in deciding on June 2, 2006, the lawsuit against PF brought by Americans United for Separation of Church and State. The judge declared unconstitutional the InnerChange Freedom Initiative in Iowa, a program started by PF.

Startlingly, the judge devoted a dozen pages to analyzing evangelicalism and PF's statement of faith, apparently determined to separate evangelicals from other Christians. Evangelicalism, he wrote, is "quite distinct from other self-described Christian faiths, such as Roman Catholicism, Mormonism, and Greek Orthodoxy." It is also "distinct from other . . . Christian denominations, such as Lutheran, United Methodist, Episcopalian, and Presbyterian."

Evangelical Christianity, he found, tends to be "anti-sacramental," downplaying "baptism, holy communion or Eucharist, marriage, [and] ordination" as "appropriate ways to interact or meet with God." (The charge of downplaying baptism will surprise my twenty million fellow Baptists.) Moreover, we are "contemptuous" of Roman Catholic practices, a conclusion sure to amuse my colleagues with Evangelicals and Catholics Together.

To sum up: evangelicals are a fringe cult inherently discriminatory, coercive, and antagonistic to other Christians.

Ironically, just days after the judge's decision, the Commission on Safety and Abuse in America's Prisons reported a desperate need in prisons for "highly structured programs which reduce misconduct in correctional facilities and lower recidivism rates after release."

This is precisely what InnerChange did. It had a proven record of rehabilitation—8 percent recidivism for graduates, according to a University of Pennsylvania study of a similar program in Texas. This compares with more than 60 percent recidivism nationally. The commission understands the urgency of these programs, because in any given year, over 600,000 prisoners will be released. Within three years, more than two-thirds will be rearrested.

Bad enough that the judge ordered closed a program that had proven successful, imperiling thousands of faith-based programs. Even worse, he expanded the Supreme Court precedent in *Lemon v. Kurtzman*. (In *Lemon v. Kurtzman* [1971] the Supreme Court struck down a Pennsylvania law allowing the state to reimburse private schools for books on secular subjects and a percentage of salaries of teachers in those schools who taught secular subjects.)

A careful reading of his opinion leads to the conclusion that even if state funds are not involved, any close government cooperation with "pervasively sectarian" groups is unconstitutional. Such a broad standard could easily be applied to church services or evangelistic events not only in prisons, but also in hospitals, military bases, or any government facility.

But the most alarming question is why the judge chose to write a sociological analysis of evangelicalism—something I've never seen before in any case. And why would he so inaccurately characterize evangelicals as a fringe cult? After all, we make up between 33 and 40 percent of the American population, drawing from scores of denominations, including many millions of Catholics.

Whatever the reason, by distinguishing evangelicals from all other Christian groups, Judge Pratt supported his finding that we discriminate and coerce conversions—despite the fact that every inmate testifying in the trial denied any coercion. Inner-Change is voluntary; at any time, inmates can drop out. Many participants are not Christians.

Judge Pratt's ruling survived appeal, enshrining in federal law a definition of evangelicals as a narrow, mean-spirited minority. This ruling can now be cited in cases where pastors publicly denounce homosexuality or pray in Jesus' name on public property. What will prevent a court from deciding what is and is not legitimate theology, according to the trendiest, most politically correct standards?

## OUR OVERSTEPPING COURTS

The first line of deterrence against the growing tyranny of our overstepping courts is the U.S. Congress. Unless Congress resists the courts' increasing expansion of power, it will be reduced to the role of traffic cop, merely making procedural laws to enforce what the courts say. And America will degenerate into what Harvard professor Michael Sandel calls a "procedural republic," where our laws no longer reflect a moral consensus but consist merely of pragmatic rules for managing the body politic.

If the representative branch of government is denied the right to reflect the people's moral vision in substantive laws, the moral underpinnings essential to a free society will be eroded.

It is time to vindicate the right of the people, acting through their representatives, to have a voice in determining the meaning of our fundamental law. This means, for one thing, taking care to vote for representatives who are willing to challenge the courts with necessary laws. It also means electing governors and presidents who will appoint justices and judges who have demonstrated a firm commitment to the Constitution and the rights it grants to free citizens, especially as those rights concern the free exercise of religion and speech.

The church can offer a genuine alternative to the nation's growing secularism only if it remains free to preach its own distinctive message, not shackled to a politically correct agenda by activist judges. As cultural trends shift and people search for spiritual answers, it would be tragic if the courts were the major stumbling block in their way.

Hopefully, there will be an outcry from Christians against the decisions of the courts that disparage evangelicals and restrict religious freedom. Courts are not always indifferent to public attitudes, as we saw in the assisted-suicide case in 1997 (*Washington v. Glucksberg*). We have to appeal and fight these repressive decisions. But in the process, evangelicals need to do some sober soul searching. For the various judges' opinions recounted in this chapter are but reflections of how many see us: coercive and bigoted.

The critical question is, do we play into the stereotypes, or do we reflect our rich heritage of abolishing the slave trade, defending human rights, and founding hospitals? These and subsequent cases present a challenge to define and defend evangelicalism, no less before the bar of public opinion than before the bar of justice.

# 9

## THE VALUE OF VIRTUOUS GOVERNMENT

# 9

# THE VALUE OF
# VIRTUOUS GOVERNMENT

The subprime mess has shaken financial markets worldwide; it's the deepest crisis since the Great Depression.[1] Millions have lost their homes to foreclosure; the unemployment rate climbed from 5.7 percent in August 2008 to hover near 10 percent at the beginning of 2011. Great Wall Street institutions have collapsed, sinking the Dow Jones and plunging world markets into chaos. Western governments have injected massive amounts of capital into their banks.

The government is surely responsible in large part for this financial chaos: Congress was grossly negligent, milking Fannie Mae and Freddie Mac for multimillion-dollar patronage jobs and forcing them to give shaky mortgages to unqualified borrowers. Now these agencies, which went private in the 1960s after being launched by the federal government in the 1930s, are under the conservatorship of the Federal Housing Finance Agency. So reform is desperately needed (if only Congress could reform itself).

As a result of these obvious examples of congressional irresponsibility, the public has lost confidence in government. By the end of 2010 a Rasmussen poll showed that the congressional approval rating had plummeted to 13 percent.[2] Our current financial mess, unsettling as it is, is only one reason for the public's loss of confidence in Washington. Space will not allow us to examine them all, but it may be instructive to look briefly at a couple of others that figure prominently in the public's mind.

## PANDER POLITICS

Campaign rhetoric today scrupulously avoids great issues, and the candidates' increasing reliance on polls and focus groups stifles genuine debate. But the deeper concern is that such poll-driven elections threaten to change the nature of government from deliberative republicanism to passive consumerism.

Campaign promises are a venerable American tradition, but now they have become the campaign. Candidates typically argue over who can better micromanage education, how to make taxpayers pay for other people's goods and services, what kind of accounting fiction can best guard Social Security, and whose tax plan would benefit whom. Grave issues like missile defense, international trade, questions of human life, the role of the courts, human rights, and "civil unions" are addressed only in passing. Computer technology profiles swing voters in battleground states so that campaign messages are precisely targeted.

One might think poll-driven campaigning the purest form of democracy, but it is the system the Founders feared most. They chose a *representative* system—a republic, not a democracy.

They envisioned a majority rule that is tempered by a deliberative process. Such a system assumes representatives will have the character to rise above public passions and do right. For example, when Abraham Lincoln and Stephen Douglas held their great debates, they weren't trolling for votes among the rank-and-file. The two were debating because the issues needed airing, and people flocked to hear them.

U.S. Senators were chosen by state legislatures until 1913, when the 17th Amendment made them electable directly by the people, thus turning them into representatives with longer terms and bigger egos. A victory for popular democracy? Maybe. But one wonders if it is a coincidence that the federal government began to expand dramatically at the expense of the states after 1913.

The overt pandering of today's political candidates clearly shows that our biblical-republican roots are withering. A generation ago, I sat at a president's side trying to end an unpopular war honorably. For four years, he had to go against the polls. What hope is there that today's politicians will do that? How does a poll-driven president summon the electorate to the routine burdens of citizenship, let alone heroic efforts?

We have chosen our last few presidents, not because they were persuasive on great issues, but because they promised wealth transfers to key constituencies and posed little threat to the comfort of everyone else. This brings to mind the scene in Dostoyevsky's *The Brothers Karamazov* of the "Grand Inquisitor." The Inquisitor, the devil incarnate, tells the returning Christ to go away because the people do not want what he is offering. They want bread, the satisfaction of their lower appetites. If the political debate is to be elevated in America, Christians will have to insist that bread alone does not satisfy the natural man, much less the spiritual man.

## THE EARMARK EPIDEMIC

Not in the fifty years I've been in Washington have I witnessed the stranglehold special interest groups now have on our political system.

In Fairmont, West Virginia, a new Institute for Scientific Research sits in what used to be a pasture. This "research center," which cost taxpayers $103 million, boasts a swimming pool, sauna, and spa. It's nearly empty and likely to stay that way. A ranking member of Congress who snuck funding for it into a law underwent investigation.

Then there's the Florida resort town called Treasure Island, which wanted $15 million to rebuild a crumbling bridge. City officials hired a lobbyist buddy of a Florida congressman, then chairman of the appropriations committee. The congressman delivered special appropriations, not for $15 million, but for $50 million. Clearly, the real Treasure Island is Washington's K Street, where lobbyists work—4,000 of them, according to journalist John Fund.

Like the Institute for Scientific Research, Treasure Island's bridge was funded through earmarks. Members of Congress add these expenditures, which bypass the budgeting process and earn approval without debate. Since 2005, earmarks cost have cost taxpayers $142.5 billion dollars. Many are infamous—like Alaska's "bridge to nowhere."

Earmarks have become an epidemic. So have Washington lobbyists. For communities, police, and firefighters, lobbyists are worth their weight in gold—or pork. For example, in one year the city of Portland, Oregon, spent $1.2 million on lobbyists and received $94 million in earmarked funds—a handsome return.

Powerful special interests have become, in effect, a fourth branch of government, spreading government largesse. The tragedy is not only that billions are being misspent, but that the priority of government is being skewed. Many lawmakers see their roles more as pandering to pressure groups than promoting the common good.

The idea of advancing the common good was central to the nation's founding fathers. In "Federalist Paper No. 10," James Madison identifies the critical question for any society: how do you assure that private factions do not undermine the public good?

"By a faction, I understand a number of citizens . . . who are united and actuated by some common impulse of passion, or of interest, adverse to the rights of other citizens or to the permanent and aggregate interests of the community," Madison wrote.

The founders built checks and balances into the Constitution, as Madison wrote, to "pit ambition against ambition and make it impossible for any elements of government to obtain unchecked power." Precisely what we see in earmarks.

Madison echoed the great Western philosophers throughout history. Aristotle believed the common good was served by individuals acting virtuously and by government providing a stable environment for its citizens. Augustine defined the common good as ordered harmony among citizens, as well as between the government and the people. "The common good of the state cannot flourish unless the citizens be virtuous, at least those whose business it is to govern," Aquinas later wrote.

Today, lobbyists and politicians have replaced the question of how to promote the common good with another question: "What's in it for me?"

## THE ROOTS OF GOVERNMENT DYSFUNCTION

This plummeting of virtue and ethics in government results directly from modern relativism, the loss of an overarching moral consensus and its replacement by private choice. Without some agreed-upon public standard, societies atomize into a thousand ideological factions, all of which fight for their own particular interests. The *Planned Parenthood v. Casey* (1992) decision expressed the underlying philosophy: everyone has the "right to define one's own concept of existence, of meaning, of the universe, and of the mystery of human life."

With that yardstick, how could we ever agree on the public good? No wonder people see government as the dispenser of goods. K Street is the ultimate corruption—those who deliver the goods for a price.

To see how moral failures and following false worldviews create crises and chaos, let's go back to the financial and credit crisis of 2008.

The roots of that crisis went beyond political blunders to Wall Street, which devised a clever new product: buy mortgages from banks, bundle them into mortgage-based securities, and sell them. Wall Street bankers reaped a windfall, but the scheme shifted the risk from the lending bank or mortgage broker to some Swiss hedge fund. Unintended consequences quickly followed. With cash flooding into the banks (which had no risks), every savings and loan, Internet start-up, lender, and mortgage broker urged people to take mortgages whether they could repay them or not.

The result: many who could not afford a home were taken in. They knew they could pay the low interest rates for the first two years, and were assured that if they could not pay higher rates once those kicked in, they could sell their houses, which were supposed to have risen in value. Everything worked so long as home prices kept rising. When they stopped rising, the scheme collapsed.

Individuals, having collectively run up trillions in debt and a zero rate of savings, share much of the blame—but no one accepted responsibility. When the meltdown started in October of 2008, the culprits in Congress feigned surprise; the public flooded them with e-mails opposing the bailout, half of them (according to polls) because they didn't feel responsible. So much for the public good.

This is dramatic evidence that worldviews do matter. The dominant attitude of recent decades says there are no moral truths—that we should simply live for the moment and get whatever we can out of life. This worldview has led to the chaos we are experiencing. By contrast, the Christian worldview teaches us to live within our means, defer gratification, and treat others honorably—all requirements for sustaining personal prosperity and the free-market system.

But free markets can remain free only if individuals behave

responsibly and police themselves. We are not doing that today; we have ignored moral restraints, even labeling them intolerant.

This financial crisis was in reality a crisis of character. And the taxpayers are stuck with a staggering bill and a shaky economic future.

The long-term casualty of this debacle is freedom. When free societies abuse their freedom, governments step in. In the wake of the meltdown, the government announced that in the future, mortgages could not be granted unless there was a written record proving the borrower had the ability to repay the loan. How comical it is that simple common sense now has to be written into law.

I pray that the government will come to its senses and bring stability back to the economy and responsibility back to government. Band-Aids won't do. We need a complete overhaul of our national priorities. But we Christians have an even bigger job. Unless we can renew in our culture a worldview encouraging virtue and responsibility, the current crisis of confidence in government is sure to grow even worse.

## THE VITAL ROLE OF CHRISTIANS

The performance of government will only change if politicians who brazenly pander to constituents in exchange for power find themselves out of work. Christians ought to press lawmakers running for reelection on whether they will renounce earmarks, quit pandering to constituencies, and act solely on the principle of what is best for the people.

But Christians also need to persuade their neighbors about the need to abandon "What's in it for me?" in favor of "What is good for all?" and to restore a common moral consensus. For Aquinas correctly reminds us that it is not possible to be truly virtuous unless we honor the needs of the whole society.

We Christians have political clout because millions of Americans share our moral concerns. But that can never be the basis of our political stance. We contend for certain truths in the political arena precisely because they are true, and because these transcendent truths are crucial to public justice and freedom.

Our message is *not*, "We put you in office, now pay up." Rather it is: "This should be done because it is right; it is a principle that undergirds any well-ordered civil society." We must be clear that the moral positions we urge are not partisan; they apply to Democrats and Republicans alike.

Our principles are derived from Scripture, but in a pluralistic society they must be translated into terms nonbelievers can understand, language that appeals to the objective moral order recognized by the ethical systems of all great civilizations—what C. S. Lewis called "the Way" or "the Tao."

For example, when we work to change abortion laws, we appeal not only to divine revelation but also to the most fundamental duty of government: to defend the defenseless. Our nation was founded by a generation willing to fight and die for the "inalienable" right to life. Both Christian believer and Enlightenment deist agreed on the rights that government must protect.

Or consider assisted suicide and eugenics. The reason we oppose legalization is that these things are contrary to the fundamental duty of government recognized since our founding. As G. K. Chesterton writes, eugenics "is chiefly a denial of the Declaration of Independence. It urges that so far from all men being born equal, numbers of them ought not to be born at all."

When we oppose so-called gay marriage and domestic-partner laws, our purpose is not to punish homosexuals but to preserve the unique legal status of the heterosexual family. This is not some theocratic power grab; it is asking government to recognize a fundamental social pattern that has undergirded every successful society throughout history.

In seeking limits on government, our motivation stems from a rich tradition of political philosophy rooted in the Reformation—a tradition that made constitutional democracy possible. It rests on the recognition that every sphere of society has its own function, its own authority, which government may not usurp but rather must protect. Dutch statesman Abraham Kuyper coined the phrase "sphere sovereignty" to assert that the individual, family, church, school, and business enterprise all owe their origin to God, not government. Therefore, their proper function and structure comes from God; there are lines that government may not cross in its social-engineering schemes.

As Kuyper put it, we live *coram Deo* (before the face of God), and we are directly responsible to God in each area of life. For Christians, politics is the high calling of ensuring that government protects the prepolitical institutions and preserves the moral order.

This is why it is so crucial not to allow ourselves to be tucked into any party's hip pocket, or cast as just another political interest group in the ideological struggle. Our concern is on a higher level: that all spheres of society are free to fulfill their God-ordained function. At times we may represent a majority, at other times only a small percentage of the vote, as in the early abolitionist movement. But our position remains the same: that there exists a natural order that government is morally obligated to respect.

Our task is to serve as society's conscience, seeing all of life from God's perspective and interpreting that vision in prudential terms for our fellow citizens. We don't seek power; we seek a society where government promotes justice in all spheres of society and protects the public good.

Given the importance of Christian influence in a just society, I have been surprised by the number of Christians who have given up on politics. "I don't like either candidate, so I'm staying home," some say. I get fed up with the vain posturing and empty promises, too. But not voting is not an option—it's both our civic and sacred duty. Voting is required of us as good citizens and as God's agents for appointing leaders.

How do we go about choosing the best candidates? Not by pulling a partisan lever—that's knee-jerk ideology. Christians live instead by revealed truth, never captive to any party. Thus, the best place to go for wisdom is not the candidates' websites, but the Bible.

Moses' father-in-law, Jethro, advised him to appoint as rulers "able men" who "fear God, men who are trustworthy and who hate a bribe." The standard is competence and integrity. Later, God ordered Samuel to pick Saul, who "shall save my people from the hand of the Philistines." This passage reminds us of Paul's teaching in Romans: government's role is to wield the sword to preserve order and restrain evil. So we should seek leaders best able to do that and to pursue justice.

Today, God no longer chooses our leaders directly (although some of us wish he did, if only to spare us the years-long political campaigns). We live in a democracy, so God entrusts to us the job of choosing leaders he will anoint. (Deuteronomy 1:12–13 shows us that democratic principles go directly back to the Old Testament.) Like Samuel, we are commissioned to choose leaders of competence, virtue, and character. That's why not voting or rejecting candidates because they are not perfect on some biblical or political score sheet is a dereliction of our trust. So is voting for a candidate simply because he is a Christian—startling as this may sound. Rather than checking on the candidates' denomination, we should look for the ablest candidate.

In casting a vote, judgment should ultimately be guided by what we perceive to be the common good, a term not often heard in today's special interest–charged political debates.

If we look at politics from God's perspective, we see that he has a deep and abiding interest in all people being treated fairly. If God favors any "special interest group," it is the poor, the hungry, the unborn, the handicapped, the prisoner—those with the least access to political power.

This is why we Christians should never allow ourselves to be, as the news media has often characterized us, just another special interest group pleading for our agendas only. But if we were a special interest group, we would be lobbying for the dignity of all, especially those who can't always speak for themselves. So maybe a particular candidate isn't going to cut your taxes or vote for your favorite program, but the real question is, will he serve all the people, or only the loudest?

After considering these criteria, if you are still tempted to stay home on Election Day, dust off your copy of *The City of God*, in which Augustine introduces us to the idea that we live in both the City of God and the City of Man. In describing them, he reiterated Jesus' teaching that while Christians live in the City of Man, they do not belong to it. We are like sojourners in a foreign country; our true home is the City of God.

But Augustine also taught that if we are to enjoy the blessings of the City of Man, we must assume the obligations of citizenship. Instead of doing our civic duty out of compulsion, the Christian does it gladly, out of obedience to God and love of neighbor.

Augustine's teaching also helps us to put the outcomes of elections into perspective. Some will be jubilant over the outcome, others bitterly disappointed. But regardless of the returns, the City of God endures. When Augustine was informed that his beloved city of Rome was in flames, his response was that the City of Man is built by man and can be destroyed by man, but the City of God is built by God and cannot be destroyed.

On Election Day we should be the best of citizens, voting for the candidate best for *all* the people. And then the next day, after indulging in your celebration—or pity party—get busy working to advance God's kingdom in this earthly society.

# 10

# Fixing
# Fragmented Worldviews

# 10

# FIXING
# FRAGMENTED WORLDVIEWS

A few years ago a *Washington Post Magazine* feature recounted the tale of Gauvin Hughes McCullough and his deaf parents: Sharon Duchesneau, his birth mother, and Candace McCullough, his adoptive mother.[1]

The article ignited a controversy, not so much because Gauvin has two mommies—sadly, that's hardly news anymore—but because Duchesneau and McCullough went out of their way to see that their child had what most people would consider a serious disability. The pair recruited a deaf friend as a sperm donor in the hope their son would be born deaf.

Several months after Gauvin's birth, an audiologist confirmed the "good" news: the baby was indeed deaf. The mothers were elated.

Why would parents, especially ones who have themselves experienced the challenges of being deaf, wish this condition on their child? After all, Gauvin already faces challenges aplenty simply because he'll grow up in a lesbian household.

The answer lies in the way that many deaf people (and others with disabilities) view themselves. Increasingly, they see deafness with a capital D—not as a disability but as a culture. They regard treatments for deafness, such as Cochlear implants, as a kind of cultural genocide.

Turning disabilities into culture may seem absurd, but the story of Gauvin Hughes McCullough is merely the *reductio ad absurdum* of the worldviews that define our age. These worldviews, collectively known as postmodernism, deny that truth corresponds to reality. Truth is simply one's subjective preference. But if reality is essentially unknowable, how do individuals make sense of the world? Certainly not by recourse to universally applicable ideas about good and evil and about the meaning of human existence. Instead, the sources for what one sociologist calls the "webs of significance" are to be found through association with a particular group, which exhibits some common identity. That group identity then defines one's meaning for life and provides the basis to negotiate with those in power.

The result of this process is ever-increasing fragmentation of our culture into smaller (and often angrier) groups. The goal of what Princeton professor Cornell West calls the "cultural politics of difference," a.k.a., identity politics, is the trashing "of the monolithic and homogeneous in the name of diversity, multiplicity, and heterogeneity."

This may sound like idle ivory-tower chatter, but the practical consequences of these ideas litter the cultural landscape. Americans are increasingly identifying with whatever group or subgroup empowers them to pursue their particular set of goals and grievances—be they deaf, gay, deaf *and* gay, or members of a particular race or sex.

This explains why, after publication of the controversial *Post* article, many defended the deaf lesbian parents. When I did a *BreakPoint* broadcast critical of parents deliberately designing disabilities for their kids, I received calls and letters accusing me of insensitivity.

I confess, I might be insensitive out of ignorance; I have never experienced what the deaf experience. But I'm not unfamiliar with or insensitive to disabilities. My daughter, Emily, is a single mom who is heroically raising Max, my autistic grandson. Max is an unusually loving kid and a special blessing. Emily loves him just as he is. But if there were a cure, Emily would, for Max's sake, grab it in a heartbeat.

Many people today, in what seems like enlightened diversity, fail to see that the behavior of Gauvin's parents reflects deep despair: despair that people from different groups can ever communicate fully with one another, and despair about the possibility of finding meaning apart from one's own little group.

This ever-increasing fragmentation of culture into smaller groups has roots in the worldview largely adopted by most of the West today. The trashing "of the monolithic and homogeneous in the name of diversity, multiplicity, and heterogeneity" may result in clans, but the tendency it demonstrates toward fragmentation has its roots in a growing descent into individualism that lacks commitment to anything outside the self. It was focus on self instead of commitment to the welfare of others that led Duchesneau and McCullough to deliberately inflict their own disability on another person. This self-focused worldview is leading to an ever-increasing fragmentation that does not stop with subdividing people into narrow clans of shared identification.

It goes on to separate individuals into isolated islands, insulated by vast seas of selfishness from commitment to others.

In Chapter 6, I mentioned sociologist Robert Bellah's extensive interviews to understand what "habits of the heart" defined average Americans. Many had no sense of community or social obligation. They even seemed to have lost the language to express commitment to anything besides themselves. Bellah saw how this attitude would, in time, unravel the church and larger society. Since then, we've seen an almost uninterrupted march toward self-focus, affecting all of our institutions but especially crippling work, marriage, and family.

Studies back up Bellah's observation that today's young adults are far less willing to commit to anything. In 2008, more than half of people ages twenty to twenty-four had been with their current employer for less than a year. Young adults are still floundering when it comes to embracing a calling. Marriage, especially, has suffered; according to U.S. Census data, young adults are marrying later than ever. A 2006 PBS documentary, *Generation Next*, gave some insight into why: desire for adventure, career advancement, and prolonged adolescence. Lack of commitment is also hitting religion—hard. Studies suggest that the iPod generation is choosing which aspects of the faith to adopt to create their own unique spiritual playlists.

Among today's young adults, the unwillingness to commit is alarming, clearly one result of the philosophies of the '60s and '70s coming to full flower.

The basic building blocks of society simply erode without commitment. Any sensible society must address this problem by educating people that commitment is the very essence of human relationships. At the least, we need to teach this in our churches. How can you begin as a Christian without death to self and total commitment to Jesus Christ? Certain characteristics are so inherent to Christianity that to neglect them is to become a walking oxymoron. A Christian without commitment is such an oxymoron.

What makes the refusal to commit beyond one's clan or self-interests so serious is that it creates problems not confined merely to groups or individuals. The ripple effect impacts society at large, fragmenting the family, driving a wedge between men and women, and creating a need for costly political solutions. For example, the widespread breakdown of marriage and family has left increasing numbers of women without adequate economic support. Which in turn, Stephen Stark writes in the *Atlantic Monthly*, has "led more women than men to be dependent on and supportive of government welfare programs." Susan Cullman of Republican Coalition for Choice puts it concretely: When you start cutting social programs, men think of getting government off their back; but women think, "My goodness, *I* might need that someday."

This gender gap illustrates what has become a familiar pattern: a political issue that turns out to be at root a moral issue. The sexual revolution promised liberation from traditional morality, but the only folks liberated were men. They were freed from family responsibilities, while women were driven into dependency on Uncle Sam. We could even say the gender gap is a measure of the degree to which women have lost confidence that husbands and fathers will stick around.

The growth of government will never be tamed unless we

first call men to examine their hearts and ask whether they are fulfilling their duties to their own families and communities. Churches need to preach once again a full biblical message on manhood: that men are called to fulfill an office as moral and spiritual head of the home. That maintaining a family is not "women's work," it is a man's job. That family-related concerns such as education and health care are not only "women's issues," they are also part of men's civic duty as custodians of their communities. It all comes down to the need for a turnaround in one's worldview, which I will address below.

If government has a role to play, it is to reinforce, not substitute for, the moral responsibility of fathers—for example, by pursuing initiatives, as some states are doing, to reverse no-fault divorce. For if men do not uphold a moral standard in their own lives—staying married, raising their children, supporting elderly parents—they are contributing to inexorable social pressures to expand the welfare state.

Overcoming the growing fragmentation in relationships between men and women requires a big change in men's hearts. When the church preaches the whole counsel of God, then believers may lead the way in restoring civic community from the ground up—beginning with families.

## The Joy of Commitment

Beyond the ramifications for society as a whole, beyond the healing of cultural fragmentation, even beyond the obvious necessity of Christian commitment, when we refuse to commit, we miss out on one of the great joys of life. When we obsess over ourselves or our narrow clans of shared self-interests, we lose the meaning of life, which is to know and serve God and love and serve our neighbors. This was made clear when thirty-three research scientists investigated the relationship between human development and community in a 2003 report, *Hardwired to Connect.* Their research revealed that we are biologically primed to find meaning through relationships.

After nearly eight decades of living, I can vouch for this. My single greatest joy is giving myself to others and seeing them grow in return. You cannot discover that without commitment. I first learned it by watching my parents care for my dying grandparents in our home. This is a custom long forgotten today, when such care is subcontracted out. I later saw it in the Marine Corps. You cannot go into combat, commanding forty-five men, as I was trained to do, if you aren't committed to one another. You are going to die if the man next to you does not cover your back.

That's a point driven home in the excellent 2010 book *Joker One,* by Donovan Campbell. It should be required reading for every Christian, because the kind of commitment you see in the platoon—Campbell calls it love for one another—is what needs to be happening in churches. Finally, I see it at this point in my life, when my greatest reward is seeing ex-convicts restored and people I've taught begin to understand the faith in its fullness.

By abandoning commitment, our narcissistic culture has lost the one thing it desperately seeks: happiness. Without commitment, our individual lives will be barren and sterile. Without commitment, our lives will lack meaning and purpose. After all, if nothing is worth dying for (the anthem of the '60s anti-war protesters), then nothing is worth living for. But with commitment comes the flourishing of society—of calling, of marriage, of the church—and of our hearts. It's the paradox Jesus so often shared when he bid us to come and die that we might truly live.

## THE SOLUTION: ADOPTING THE CORRECT WORLDVIEW

The sad case of the deaf lesbians and their deaf-by-design baby and the individualistic self-focus of postmodernity shows us clearly why American society is fragmenting into narrow clans and narrower selves. But these trends also offer Christians an apologetics opportunity: we must show why postmodern relativism is the cause of such despair and is at the root of much cultural restlessness and fragmentation. And then we must point the way out of the corner that postmoderns have painted themselves into.

Christianity acknowledges the differences between groups and individuals—but it also provides a basis for transcending those differences. While Christianity in Guatemala is different from Christianity in Grand Rapids, it is clearly the same faith. It's a faith that offers joyous hope—both eternally and in the here and now. And it doesn't demand the crassest form of self-centeredness: deliberately visiting one's disadvantages on one's children.

Christianity ends fragmentation by providing the only worldview that conforms to reality. It is the only worldview that, instead of separating clans and individuals into isolated and self-enclosed units, brings them together in a transcendent unity. To help readers understand and apply this worldview to the needs of contemporary society, let's look briefly at its central features.

Genesis 1 teaches that on the first five days, God did the work of creating directly. But on the sixth day, he formed human beings in his image to carry on his creative work, commanding them to fill and subdue the earth. This is the "cultural commission," and it is just as binding as the Great Commission. It means we must go beyond personal conversion and develop a faith that encompasses every part of life—every sphere of work, every aspect of the world.

In short, a worldview.

Developing a worldview is not some ivory-tower exercise; it is crucial for everything we do. Take the realm of personal life and moral choices. Since every choice we make—who we marry, what career we aspire to, how we raise our kids—reflects our beliefs about reality, having the right worldview is essential for the proper ordering of our lives. If we don't understand God's created purpose, both moral and physical, then we will live like a person who walks into a room blindfolded and bumps his shins against the furniture.

Second, worldview is important for apologetics. What happens when your children come home from school with challenges to their faith raised in science class? Can you explain to a skeptical neighbor the problem with moral relativism? Believers today face a clash of worldviews, and it is imperative that we learn to recognize and analyze what is false. Unless we know the biblical approach to science and ethics, to law and the arts, we have no defense against contrary ideas.

Third, having a complete worldview is crucial for evangelism. When Paul addressed the Greeks on Mars Hill, he framed the gospel in a context they could understand, quoting their own poets. And he did not begin with the message of salvation, he began with Creation: "The God who made the world and everything in it is the Lord of heaven and earth" (Acts 17:24). Paul argued that even the Greeks, though unschooled in Scripture, ought to know that God is no golden idol. Since he created us, he must be a personal being—and thus someone to whom we are personally accountable. Only after establishing who God is did Paul preach about the Resurrection. This is the approach we must take in our modern Athens, starting with Creation, and only then explaining the Fall and redemption.

Indeed, these are the same basic elements that every worldview must have: *Creation*—Where did we come from? *Fall*—What's wrong with the world? Why is there evil and suffering? *Redemption*—What's the solution, and how can we build a better world? And *meaning*—What's my purpose in life?

By comparing worldviews on each point, we can show that only Christianity offers a consistent, rational answer—one that fits the real world.

Knowing, teaching, and reflecting this accurate worldview in your own life is the key to reviving our witness in today's culture. And it's the key to reversing today's cultural fragmentation. Many Christians are discouraged by a sense that we are losing the "culture war," and they talk about withdrawing. But one reason we have not been more effective is that we have a truncated view of Christianity. We must understand that we are engaged in a great conflict of worldviews, and we cannot contend with anything less than a comprehensive biblical worldview.

Paradoxically, the note of despair is being sounded just as the American people are awakening to the failures of postmodernity. This change is offering us the greatest opportunity in generations. An NBC-*Wall Street Journal* poll uncovered a startling turn-around in attitudes: 84 percent of self-described conservatives and 33 percent of liberals say that what's "important for society" today is to "promote respect for traditional values." People are realizing that the prevailing worldviews fail to provide a basis for a safe and stable public order.

Surely this is no time to withdraw. Instead, we must seize the opportunity to demonstrate that Christianity gives the only rational, coherent framework for public and private life and, indeed, for all reality—because it begins with the God who is the sovereign Creator of all.

This is a message our fragmented world yearns to hear.

# 11

## TURNING
## THE CHURCH AROUND

# 11

# TURNING

## THE CHURCH AROUND

Have evangelicals come full circle in just fifty years—from fundamentalist isolation to mainstream acceptance?[1] Have we embraced a national creed that values personal growth over doctrinal orthodoxy?

Unhappily, one of America's most insightful observers says that's precisely what we've done. Conservative columnist David Brooks of the *New York Times* argues that Americans no longer take religious doctrines seriously. We assume religious differences are temporary, that denominational distinctions will fade away, and "We will all be united in God's embrace."

This comforting assumption means that millions feel free to try on different denominations (as several presidential candidates have done), and we're inclined to think all people of goodwill are "basically on the same side," Brooks writes. As evidence, he cites President Bush's comment that Christians and Muslims pray to the same God—an assertion that is "theologically controversial, but . . . faithful to the national creed."

The result, says Brooks, is a religion that is easygoing and experiential rather than rigorous and intellectual. To fill their pews, Brooks writes, pastors "emphasize the upbeat and the encouraging and play down the business of God's wrath." In modern "seeker sensitive" churches, "the technology is cutting edge, the music is modern, the language is therapeutic, the dress is casual."

This easygoing attitude, combined with a belief in holy homogenization, is why Christians have difficulty sustaining culture war efforts, Brooks maintains—and why fire-and-brimstone groups like the Moral Majority and the Christian Coalition dissolved or became "husks of their former selves." Evangelicals are, he concludes, quoting sociologist Alan Wolfe, "part of mainstream culture, not dissenters from it."

Brooks' column set me back on my heels. If he's right, it's a devastating indictment of the church. Is it really possible that we've become mainstream?

I didn't want to believe it, but after discussing the column with friends, and studying the latest and most depressing data from the Barna Group, I realized that Brooks—standing on the outside peering into our high-tech sanctuaries—may see evangelicals more realistically than we see ourselves.

At least two evangelical luminaries have written articles with a whiff of resignation, explaining that, after all, we shouldn't expect to transform the surrounding culture; it has always been hostile to evangelicals and always will be, so we should just hunker down. While they didn't intend it, their words can be read as an acknowledgement that we should no longer engage the culture.

This is an attractive proposition to battle-scarred cultural warriors. Just give us our lovely sanctuaries, our padded pews, and our upbeat music, and we'll no longer worry about society disintegrating around us. The culture will ignore us, and we'll ignore the culture, which will be nice when we socialize with nonbelievers who will no longer consider us backwoods fundamentalists trying to impose our morality on them.

That's the definition of "mainstream": to get along. To get there, all we have to do is abandon biblical responsibility.

## How Entertainment Trumps Content

Nowhere is this trend toward cultural accommodation more evident than in contemporary Christian music. Both in our worship services and on Christian radio, the move toward entertaining music and the rationales given for it provide clear insight into the way Christians are now thinking.

When church music directors lead congregations in singing contemporary Christian music, I often listen stoically with teeth clenched. But one Sunday morning, I cracked. We'd been led through endless repetitions of a meaningless ditty called "Draw Me Close to You," which has zero theological content and could just as easily be sung in any nightclub. When I thought it was finally and mercifully over, the music leader beamed. "Let's sing that again, shall we?" he asked. "No!" I shouted, loudly enough to send heads all around me spinning while my wife, Patty, cringed.

I admit I prefer traditional hymns, but even so, I'm convinced that much of the music being written for the church today reflects an unfortunate trend—slipping across the line from worship to entertainment. Evangelicals are in danger of amusing ourselves to death, to borrow the title of the classic Neil Postman book.

This trend is evident not just in theater-like churches where musicians—with their guitars and bongo drums—often perform at ear-splitting levels. It's also true of Christian radio, historically an important source of serious preaching and teaching. Several stations recently—many acting on the advice of a leading consulting firm—have dropped serious programming in favor of all-music formats. For example, a major station in Baltimore has dropped four talk shows in order to add music. Family Life Radio, a first-class broadcaster, has adopted a new program split of 88 percent music "to appeal to the thirty-five to fifty-year-old demographic." A respected broadcaster recently dropped *Focus on the Family* on the grounds that it had become too involved in "moral issues." Does anyone really believe the Bible is indifferent to moral questions—or that modern Christians should be?

One station canceled my four-minute *BreakPoint* commentary saying that four minutes is the equivalent of one song. Horrors! Besides, the station manager allowed, *BreakPoint* is too serious and not contemporary enough. When another major station, this one in Cincinnati, replaced *BreakPoint* with music, I called the station manager, arguing that believers need to think Christianly about major worldview issues. The young woman on the other end of the phone admonished me: "But we don't want to do anything that will upset our listeners." Younger women, she said, want "something to help them cope with life."

This view was confirmed by a Christian homemaker interviewed for a TV special on evangelicalism. She is so busy, she explained, taking care of the kids, family activities, Bible study, cooking, etc., that she doesn't even read the newspaper or care what is happening in the world around her. Church for her is getting her spirits lifted.

Admittedly, modern life does create enormous stress. But can't the church offer comfort *and* help people confront the culture?

The decision by influential Christian broadcasters and music companies to avoid moral controversies could result in the church withdrawing from the culture as it tragically did a century ago. What is the job of Christian churches or Christian radio, after all? To give people what they want, or—as with any ministry— to give them what they need? Music is important in the life of the church and can inspire us to focus on Christ. But it cannot take the place of solid teaching.

## The Abandonment of Propositional Truth

Perhaps the most critical slippage of the contemporary church is in its current de-emphasis on the core truths that support its validity. The gospel above all else is revealed propositional truth—truth that speaks to all of life. Doctrine and biblical teaching are not—as some "emerging church" advocates believe—dry, dusty, abstract notions. This truth has to be carried into the heart and applied. But there is no escaping that it is truth that must be learned.

Sure, skits and catchy music are good tools for drawing people in, and good Christian music on the radio can inspire us. But these things aren't an end in and of themselves; they should engage us in learning and applying truth.

It is clear that the emphasis of today's church on inclusion, coping with problems, and inspiring good feelings has cost us dearly in the area of learning and applying truth. In the mid-2000s, a Pew Forum on Religion and Public Life survey found rampant doctrinal ignorance among American Christians. Fifty-seven percent of evangelicals believed people who follow religions other than their own can enjoy eternal life. The results were so unexpected that Pew repeated the survey, asking more specific questions. The answers were virtually unchanged. Astonishingly, about half believed that everyone, atheists included, was going to end up in heaven. Heaven for the godless? That's the old heresy of universalism.

Indifference to the truths of the gospel is seen in many other spheres, such as among those who champion "deeds, not creeds" (I do the deeds of prison ministry *because* I believe the creeds), and in endless discussions about new ways to "understand" or "do" theology. Some embrace another old heresy, that doctrines must be extracted from inward experience—that is, personal feelings. That's a version of Gnosticism.

Still others want to make Christianity "fit" the postmodern era or "work out" their theology in public, with non-Christians helping to shape the outcome. Yes, we need to contextualize the message so that hearers in a given time and culture can grasp the truth we proclaim. But that is radically different from changing the definitive, concise summary of Christian truth the early church fathers accomplished in their councils.

As one reporter noted, even when Christians know correct doctrine, they are afraid of speaking the truth for fear of offending others. *What right have I to impose my beliefs on others?* is a thought that shapes too many of us believers.

This is why J. I. Packer, on his eightieth birthday, said that the greatest challenge of evangelicalism is to re-catechize our churches. More than ever, Christians need to be able to speak intelligently and courageously about the hope that lies within. The problem is, so many Christians no longer possess the basic knowledge of the faith or a coherent understanding of what it means to live as a Christian. While we should be ingesting the meatier doctrines and issues, we must make it our priority to go back and feed our churches on the basics—the "milk" of the Word. In other words, "We have now sunk to a depth at which restatement of the obvious is the first duty of intelligent men." Written in 1939, George Orwell's words might well be addressed to the leaders of today's biblically illiterate church.

The most obvious thing to be said about Christianity is that it rests on historic facts: the Creation, the Incarnation, and the Resurrection. Since our doctrines are truth claims, they cannot be mere symbolism.

Clearly, when we stop taking seriously the historical truths of the church, we undermine our witness. Personal faith is of course vital, but it is not sufficient. And yes, doctrine has often been taught so that it comes across as dry and dusty. But as Dorothy Sayers noted, once we grasp what Christian doctrines teach, "The Dogma is the Drama."

The determination to restore orthodox faith—the faith "that was once for all entrusted" (Jude 3)—brought about the Reformation, of which we are heirs. A new emphasis on orthodox doctrine could also transform the church and culture today.

Some years ago, I visited Athens and mounted the slippery rock called Mars Hill. At the top, I stood where I imagined

Paul had confronted the Areopagus, the wise men of the cultural center of the world. Paul challenged them by referring to their own literature and false altars, and then boldly proclaimed the gospel, concluding that God had raised Jesus from the dead. It's the same message I preach in prisons today. I think it's far more exhilarating to stand on a belief that has survived 2,000 years of persecution than to flit from one fad to another.

Few people accepted Paul's invitation that day to follow Christ. But billions have followed him ever since, because Christ has an unstoppable power. He has the power to break Satan's hold on our souls and joyfully transform our lives.

Orwell was right: in a crisis, we often have a duty to restate the obvious. We must continually remind our doctrinally confused brethren of the obvious truths of Christianity. The greatest challenge for serious Christians today is not reinventing Christianity, but rediscovering its core teachings.

A vital key to turning today's church around is taking special care to see that the next generation is solidly grounded in Christianity's core teachings and infused with an accurate worldview. Parents must not assume that simply because their kids are in Sunday school they are receiving this critical training. They must examine what our churches are teaching our kids about truth—assuming they're teaching *anything*. Youth leaders are good at activities like laser tag and Ultimate Frisbee. That's fine: draw kids in. But they must couple this with a bracing dose of worldview instruction. At the Colson Center for Christian Worldview, we have developed worldview curricula and discovered that young people hunger for it. We'd better ground our students in worldview thinking before they leave for college, where professors challenge everything they believe.

Even if our kids do get trained at church, the family must supplement it: around the breakfast table, reading devotionals that tackle worldview questions, and at other times critiquing films, analyzing the news, and unmasking unbiblical teachings in everything from popular music to television commercials.

Lay people can do this. A friend, Nancy Fitzgerald, has been teaching basic apologetics for teens in her home for years. Between 150 and 200 kids come for a lecture, then break into groups to discuss the material. They often continue the discussion later via e-mail. The results among the kids—an ability to boldly witness to the truth—have been spectacular.

Do you think I'm overstating the need for worldview training? Look around: it's impossible to disconnect kids from the culture. The idea that we can separate ourselves from our social surroundings, as Christians did a century ago, is foolish—unless we move to a desert island. We simply cannot escape the long, grubby arm of television, the Internet, music, and magazines.

Our only hope is to teach discernment. It's no coincidence that of the many groups I've spoken to in the last year, the only student who had the right worldview answers was a senior at Virginia Tech who grew up in a family that is both godly and worldly-wise.

We've no time to lose. All the evidence shows that we're already losing our kids. With only 9 percent of born-again teens believing in absolute truth, can we rescue this generation? Can we afford not to try?

## Recovering the "Cultural Commission"

Finally, the revitalization of the church will not be complete until it recovers its God-given mission to engage the culture. Christians are called to be countercultural, a force for moral change in a sinful world. But if we surrender that role, we should be forewarned: if we stop attempting to change the culture, the culture will have already changed us.

Two Christian families recently—and tragically—discovered this. Both were deeply involved in the church and homeschooled their children. Then one day, the husband from one family ran off with the wife from the other family. When shocked friends questioned her, the wife defiantly replied: "Don't I have a right to be happy?" It could have been a line from the postmodern film, *The Hours*, in which the central character leaves her family to find happiness. Clearly this woman, like so many, had compartmentalized her faith. God was for Sundays; secular culture shaped her worldview the rest of the week.

We must fight the temptation to treat our faith the way we treat our careers—as a source of entertainment, fulfillment, and happiness. Remember the warning of C. S. Lewis: If you're seeking happiness, don't choose Christianity, choose port wine.

When it comes to the culture, there's no such thing as peaceful coexistence. If we're not defending truth, fighting for Christian values in all of life, the truth will be sacrificed on the altar of mainstream secularism.

Does this sound like a militant call to arms? I hope so. I can think of nothing more important than proving David Brooks wrong. God will judge us harshly if we stand around enjoying the warm glow of our culture's approval—while the culture crumbles.

Just a few years ago I exhorted a gathering of pastors to engage today's cultural battles, particularly to support the Federal Marriage Amendment. Afterward, the pastors had many questions—but they were also confused.

One asked: "But won't engaging the culture this way interfere with fulfilling the Great Commission? Isn't this our job—to win people to Christ?"

That people still raise this question surprised me. "Of course we're called to fulfill the Great Commission," I replied. "But we're also called to fulfill the cultural commission." Christians are agents of God's saving grace—bringing others to Christ, I explained—but we are also agents of his common grace: sustaining and renewing his creation, defending the created institutions of family and society, critiquing false worldviews.

As I spoke, I saw the pastors' eyes light up in a great "Aha!" moment.

Understanding the cultural commission is especially critical each time we approach a decisive election. We know what a key role our elected leaders play in culture war battles. But many pastors question whether it's appropriate to urge their flocks to vote for politicians who support moral issues—or even to engage in moral debates.

As for voting, the answer is obvious. While, as I have written elsewhere, pastors should not make partisan endorsements, it is our obligation to see that Christians as good citizens vote and do so with discernment about where politicians stand on moral issues. I wish we had the courage of some of our Catholic brethren who've threatened to withhold Communion (and implicitly, votes) from those who flout biblical teaching.

As for getting involved with cultural issues, Scripture is clear, starting in Genesis. As I noted in the previous chapter, for five days, God created the universe. On the sixth day, he created human beings—and ordered them to act as agents in his ongoing work. From then on, the development of the creation would be primarily social and cultural: it would be the work humans performed as they reflected his image, exercised dominion, and obeyed his command to fill and subdue the earth.

The same command binds Christians today. We bear children, plant crops, build cities, form governments, and create works of art. While sin introduced a destructive power into God's created order, it did not obliterate that order. And when we are redeemed, we are both freed from sin and restored to do what God designed us to do: Create culture.

The Lord's cultural commission is, I believe, inseparable from the Great Commission. Every part of creation came from God's hand, every part was drawn into the mutiny of humanity against God, and every part will someday be redeemed. This means caring about all of life—redeeming people and redeeming culture. We are instructed, after all, to think biblically, taking "captive every thought to make it obedient to Christ" (2 Corinthians 10:5).

If we're tempted to ignore the great moral issues of our day, or dismiss them as "just politics," we are betraying our biblical mandate and our own heritage. Nothing could be deadlier for the church, nor for the culture, since real Christianity invariably provides a healthy influence on society.

Evangelicals must never be content with a tepid Christianity that embraces only evangelization and the "feel good" church while alien philosophies hostile to the created order hijack our culture. Look at the issues before us: so-called gay marriage—an oxymoron that will undermine the foundational institutions of society; the creation of life in man's image (cloning); abortion; terrorism driven by religious extremists; and defining "just war" in the age of terror, to name a few. Christians must boldly and confidently recommit to engaging contemporary culture with a fresh vision of hope.

Don't tell me you don't want to get your hands dirty in the grimy world of politics and cultural debate. If Christians do not seize this moment and act on the cultural commission, there soon will be no culture left to save. But when we do our duty, we can change the world. Look at Christians like William Wilberforce, who spent most of his life fighting—and winning—the war against the British slave trade. Christians at their post, doing their duty, have brought about the greatest social reforms of modern times.

What reforms will you and I be remembered for?

Each of us must work out our role in the common grace in our own lives, glorifying God by helping restore his creation—by bringing the majesty of God and his righteousness to bear against the crumbling structures of a fallen society.

# 12

# THE ULTIMATE HOPE
# FOR A DECAYING CULTURE

# 12

# THE ULTIMATE HOPE
# FOR A DECAYING CULTURE

In the weeks following the 2001 terrorist attacks on New York's World Trade Center and the Pentagon, Americans crowded into churches.[1] Many congregations rebroadcast President Bush's memorable address to Congress and gave stirring patriotic sermons. Mostly it was the right kind of civil religion, urging us to be the best of citizens wherever God places us.

We were also busy comforting the grief-stricken and reminding our leaders about Christian teaching on the just use of military force. But what was missing in the flurry of flag-waving and comfort-giving was something that should have been the church's primary task: calling itself, and then the nation, to repentance.

For years, many of us have only half-jokingly said that if God doesn't bring judgment on America soon, he'll have to apologize to Sodom and Gomorrah. Many have pointed to September 11 and subsequent disasters, such as Hurricane Katrina, the Fort Hood massacre, and the breakdown of our national economy, as warning shots foreshadowing God's impending judgment. I approach this subject gingerly because it's easy to be misunderstood, and I try to avoid end-times prophecy that makes Christians appear irrelevant to the world.

Still, the question must be asked: Can we discern God's purposes in these earthshaking events? Might God be using these attacks as a warning of impending judgment?

## DOES AMERICA DESERVE JUDGMENT?

As Charles Krauthammer wrote on Townhall.com, the obvious reasons Islam is fighting "the great jihad" against the United States are religion, ideology, political power, and territory. But "this is also about—deeply about—sex." The jihadists claim that wherever freedom travels—"especially in America and Europe—it brings sexual license and corruption, decadence and depravity."

Already in the pages of this book we have addressed many of the deep moral, cultural, economic, philosophical, and political problems that are wreaking chaos on our once-stable nation. In the face of such obvious cultural decay, how can anyone believe there is enough moral fiber left for cultural renewal? What makes us believe Christians can turn things around in the next millennium?

Admittedly, the forces arrayed on the battlefield appear overwhelmingly against us. The cultural centers of power are firmly in the grip of secularists: from Washington to Hollywood, from the media to academia. Small wonder Christians often feel lonely and isolated. But this assessment of the cultural battleground is misleading, for on our side of the lines is a power mightier than anything secularism can muster—the Spirit of him who gave Jesus Christ to our world and brought him back from the dead. This power is all that is needed to enable today's church to fulfill the mission of Christ on earth and transform our culture in a way that will reverse its present trend toward fatal decadence.

## UNDERSTANDING THE MISSION OF CHRIST

The Jews of Christ's time completely missed the point of his mission on earth. They believed the Messiah would arrive as a king on a stallion with a flashing sword. But God, who delights in confounding worldly wisdom, dealt with Satan's cruel reign with a quiet invasion of planet Earth. Instead of sending a mighty army, he chose an unknown, teenage virgin.

Thirty years after his humble birth, Jesus increased the Jews' befuddlement when he told his followers, "The time has come. . . . The kingdom of God is near. Repent and believe the good news!" (Mark 1:15). Then he read from the book of Isaiah: "The Spirit of the Lord is upon me, because he anointed me to preach the gospel to the poor . . . to proclaim release to the captives, and recovery of sight to the blind, to set free those who are oppressed" (Luke 4:18 NASB). Then Jesus closed the book and announced: "Today this Scripture is fulfilled in your hearing" (Luke 4:21). In effect, the carpenter's son had just announced that he was the king—an outrageous claim to the Jews, and so radical that people wanted to kill him that very day.

Sometimes I think Jesus' announcement of the liberation of the Jewish people and the coming of God's kingdom is as misunderstood today as it was by the Jews of his time. Christ was bringing in the reign of God on earth; first, through his own ministry, and then by establishing a peaceful occupying force—his church—which would carry on God's redeeming work until Christ's return in power and glory and the kingdom's final triumph.

As I've written in my book, *The Faith Given Once, for All*, Jesus' announcement was the decisive moment in the whole of human history. Preoccupied with self and distracted by affluence, many Christians try to confine the gospel to a superior form of therapy; they fail to see it as a cosmic plan of redemption in which they, as fallen creatures, are directly involved.

But while the average Christian may not "get" this announcement, those locked behind bars certainly do. Whenever I've preached to inmates over the past thirty-two years, I've read Jesus' inaugural sermon. When I quote his promise of freedom for the prisoners, the inmates often raise their arms and cheer. Jesus' message means freedom and victory for those who once had no hope. They aren't distracted by the encumbrance of wealth.

In more than three decades of ministry I've spoken to all kinds of crowds, but never to a more enthusiastic group than I encountered one winter in Newton, Iowa. When I finished speaking, 140 smiling men startled me by jumping to their feet. As if on command, they shouted in unison, "This is my Bible . . . a lamp unto my feet . . . a light unto my path."

With each phrase, they clutched their Bibles and thrust them heavenward. The sound reverberated off the concrete walls. A Promise Keepers meeting? Young Life? No, these were prison inmates at the dedication of a Christian program started by

Prison Fellowship. I was unprepared for such enthusiasm. The program had just opened, hardly allowing time for the men—many of whom were not Christians when they arrived—to get adjusted. Iowa, after all, is the Corn Belt, not the Bible Belt. While mixing with the men at lunch, I heard none of the customary prison griping but plenty of excitement over newfound faith. One "lifer" announced he was excited to be in prison: "I'm spending my life on a mission to win prisoners to Jesus."

I left that day with my spirit refreshed by the almost childlike faith of these men. For me the visit was like flipping through the pages of Jonathan Edwards's *Narrative of Surprising Conversions*, the classic chronicle of the Great Awakening of the 1730s. The thrill never fades when witnessing God rescuing lives from despair.

But the transformation of the prison itself was as dramatic as the change I saw in these men. Over the years, I've visited more than 600 prisons in forty countries. Most are dreary, often dirty, depressing places. Men and women shuffle around listlessly with vacant expressions and their heads down. Anger, bitterness, and corruption are prevalent; one seldom hears laughter or sees signs of mirth.

But in Newton, like at the Houston facility that hosts a similar Prison Fellowship program, the environment was totally different. The clean units reflected the pride these men take in their prison. They had a sense of purpose—people were busy with work or classes from early morning to lights out. There was little time for TV or lying around on bunks. They built community, helped one another, and willingly obeyed the rules.

I tell this story because I believe it has a much larger application. This is how a culture can be transformed. The process begins when the believers band together in a loving fellowship, a "church," really. Then they evangelize, like the inmates who invite people from other wings to revival services. Though in the minority at first, the Christian prisoners take biblical teaching to heart and boldly live it out. Others begin to follow their example and soon they reach a critical mass. In time all of the men, almost unconsciously, have adopted different standards of behavior.

What I saw that day is a metaphor of the church.

We tend to evaluate churches by the classic marks: preaching, the sacraments, and discipline. But a fourth might be added: its impact on culture. John Calvin said that the church "can never exist without bringing forth fruit and prospering by God's blessing." He meant that when the church is faithful, it impacts everyone and everything.

This is a sobering thought for today's church as we look at the cultural decay around us. It may seem a stretch to suggest that Christians could replicate in their communities what we see in these prisons. But history teaches that we can. The Great Awakening planted the seeds for our nation's independence and set the stage for the abolition of slavery.

The Welsh revival in 1904 also transformed culture, as was chronicled by historian J. Edwin Orr. During the 1905 New Year celebration, the Swansea County Police Court—for the first time ever—reported not a single arrest for drunkenness. Police complained they had nothing to do; converted gamblers reformed their ways; thieves returned stolen goods; the courts had no cases to try. Orr reported that it "even affected work, but in a surprising way. So many men had given up foul language that the pit ponies which dragged the coal trucks in the mine tunnels did not understand what was being said to them."

God's ways often confound the wisdom of the world. And that is what he seems to be doing by using society's outcasts to show the rest of us how to transform culture.

## RADICAL TRANSFORMING POWER

Perhaps the most dramatic example I've seen of how the power of Christ can transform culture occurred when I visited another prison. Jester II is a wing of a Texas prison that hosts Prison Fellowship's InterChange Freedom Initiative (IFI), where prayers have replaced early-morning pushups and group Bible studies have preempted evening MTV. The near-monastic atmosphere is especially surprising when you consider that most of the inmates who volunteer for the program are hard-core, repeat offenders.

I dropped in on a class on drug and alcohol prevention to hear one of the inmates say, "I've been in three therapy programs, and they don't work, because I'm back in prison." Then he added, "We're not interested in therapy. We're interested in transformation." The room resounded with amens. The inmates are so grateful for the chance to work on spiritual solutions to their problems that some have even voluntarily turned down parole to stay in the program—something ordinarily unheard of.

But the most breathtaking moment in my visit came during a graduation ceremony for inmates who had completed the entire eighteen-month program. As an inmate approached me for his certificate, out of the corner of my eye I saw a tall, stately woman rise from her seat among the visitors. Her name was Mrs. Washington, and she swept to the front, wrapped her arms around the inmate, and declared to everyone, "This young man is my adopted son."

The place was electrified. I saw hardened criminals and tough corrections officials with tears in their eyes, for they knew that this young man was behind bars for the murder of Mrs. Washington's daughter.

Arriving at this moment had not been easy for either of them. Ron Flowers had maintained his innocence during fifteen years in prison. After meeting with an IFI volunteer, for the first time he admitted his crime and prayed that his victim's family would forgive him.

On her side, every year of Ron's sentence Mrs. Washington had written angry letters to the parole board, urging them to deny him parole. But the same week that Ron confessed, strangely, Mrs. Washington felt an overwhelming conviction that she was to forgive the man who had murdered her daughter. The next day, she wrote the board that she no longer opposed Ron's parole. She then tracked Ron down to express her forgiveness.

Their tearful embrace at the graduation ceremony was the climax of a series of what can only be called miracles. Only the supernatural grace of God could bring together a murderer and his victim's mother; only the resurrection power of Christ can create love where there once was hatred and revenge. I know that in my own power I could never have done what this woman did.

And if a miracle can happen in prison, it can happen anywhere. God's power can penetrate the darkest corners of society bringing radical transformation. This is what we must never forget when we face the solid phalanx of a hostile culture bent on immorality and decay. Like Elisha praying that his servant would see the invisible army of angels in their chariots of fire, we must pray to see that "those who are with us are more than those who are with them" (2 Kings 6:16).

Nor does the story of Mrs. Washington end with that dramatic reconciliation. A friend was so moved that he sent her a gift of $10,000. She promptly sent some of the money to Ron Flowers to get him started in his new life out of prison, and the rest she used to set up a scholarship in her daughter's name at her church. Such generosity can only flow from a profound experience of God's redeeming grace.

So do we have reason for hope as we stand in the opening decades of the new millennium? Absolutely. The reason can be stated in three simple words: *the empty tomb*. Christ has overcome death and sin, and that same power is ours by faith.

We must overcome the temptation to despair. It's true that the forces in the culture war are not evenly matched—for we have an army of angels on our side. And those who are with us will always be far more than those who are in the world.

## TRANSFORMING OUR NATION

Let's say, for the sake of argument, that God used the September 11 attacks, Hurricane Katrina, and other disasters as signs of judgment. What will save us, then, are not the Marines, cruise missiles, satellites, smart bombs, flood controls, or government policies; the only thing that will save us is deep and genuine repentance.

Judgment always begins with God's people. So the first message of the church must point to our own need for repentance. And if we are honest, we have much to repent for; our idols look little different from the culture's.

Time after time, throughout the Old Testament, we see God's people falling into the sin of idolatry, being oppressed by their enemies, repenting, and then being delivered by God. The message is clear: we must repent for ourselves and our nation, just as Nehemiah did before God appointed him to leadership. Later he led the Jews (recently returned from Persian exile) in corporate confession and repentance. We should understand repentance as Martin Luther did—central to life in Christ.

William Wilberforce was a Christian member of Parliament who fought to abolish the slave trade in the British Empire. During a crucial moment in that campaign he said that his hope for Britain depended "not so much on her navies and armies, nor on the wisdom of her rulers, as on the persuasion that she still contains many who love and obey the gospel of Christ, that their prayers may yet prevail."

We must always be careful about how we express this to our friends. We're not blaming God for terrorist attacks or other disasters. God does not create evil, but he does use it to his purposes. That's a big difference. Though it occurred a decade ago, I've been deeply burdened since September 11. I find myself at times crying out for God's mercy—for myself, the church, my ministry, and our country.

If I am correct in thinking God may be using disastrous events to wake up America, we must face the same sobering reality Wilberforce faced. We will prevail not so much because of the efforts of our government, but only if God in his mercy decides to forgive us, heal our land, and give America another chance. This means that the role of the church is of life-and-death importance.

# 13

## THE POLITICALLY ENGAGED CHURCH

# 13

# THE POLITICALLY
# ENGAGED CHURCH

The nature of power makes government an ever-present threat to religious freedom in any nation.[1] Government appetite for power can threaten not only the church, but also other institutions and freedoms as well. Christians, with their insight into the nature of sin and how it tends to corrupt those who wield power, are in a unique position to influence a society in a way that protects these freedoms and institutions. That is why it is crucial that the church be engaged politically—not to exercise power but to protect constitutionally guaranteed freedoms.

Surely no one today is blind to the government's tendency toward expanding its power. The economic crisis that began in 2008 has fueled a rapid expansion of government control over banks and industries. And unless Congress or the courts overturn current legislation, it will soon take over health care, which alone amounts to one-sixth of America's GNP. This transfer of responsibilities raises cautionary flags, especially for Christians.

In the 1960s Jacques Ellul, the eccentric French Reformed thinker, prophesied the politicization of all aspects of life. In his prophetic book, *The Political Illusion*, he predicted the West would adopt the idea that every problem has a political solution. This, he warned, leads to increasing dependence on the state by ordinary citizens and decreasing citizen control of government.

From Kennedy's New Frontier to LBJ's Great Society to President Bush's No Child Left Behind education initiative, challengers promise new programs, and, when elected, try to deliver. The result: programs pile upon programs, agencies upon agencies, and the whole structure of government becomes so unwieldy it can hardly function. We saw this happen in the wake of Hurricane Katrina and the BP Gulf oil spill, and I fear we might see it again during another terrorist attack.

When government expands its power, the people are the ultimate losers. Virtually everybody has to deal with government, whether to obtain a driver's license or to open a business. We often end up mired in bureaucratic gridlock, even over minor issues—precisely as Ellul predicted.

Even Christians can succumb to the political illusion. Several years ago, a Christian leader blurted: "I think we have been legislated out of the possibility of a spiritual revival." Some Christians seem almost defeatist when "our" candidates lose.

But the real evil of the illusion is that it distracts us from other aspects of life. Politics are important, of course: Christians have a duty to be the best of citizens, bringing concerns of justice and righteousness into public life. The importance of being active in the political realm becomes clear when we realize that two Bush appointees to the Supreme Court made the difference in the

Court's decision to uphold the ban on partial-birth abortion. But we must keep political activity in perspective, seeing that it fulfills its proper role in what Dutch politician and church leader Abraham Kuyper labeled "sphere sovereignty"—each sphere (family, church, government) carrying out its own responsibility before God.

This means we must guard against government encroachment on other spheres and not let the political illusion blind us to what makes life rich and meaningful: family, church, and community. In short, culture.

The concept of the balance of powers comes directly from Christian doctrines. The Reformers introduced the idea of sphere sovereignty, which holds that government's role is limited so that other spheres—family, church, and voluntary associations—are free to exercise their authority. Similarly, Catholic social teaching embraced the principle of subsidiarity, arguing that services should be delivered by the agencies closest to recipients.

In both traditions, the state's power is limited by intermediate structures, which act as brakes on all-powerful government. But the expanding reach of government can threaten voluntary associations, what English philosopher Edmund Burke called "the little platoons."

For instance, in establishing the new White House Office of Faith-based and Neighborhood Partnerships, President Obama did not include the Bush-era tacit exemption from federal non-discrimination in hiring requirements for faith-based ministries. Joshua DuBois, who heads the office, said they will handle this issue on a case-by-case basis while deciding whether to change federal rules. Sounds reasonable—but who would risk money and credibility on an outreach program that may later be deemed illegal?

Moreover, many AIDS shelters and homeless facilities are run by Catholic Charities and the Salvation Army, which depend partly on government funds. But if the Obama administration orders these groups to hire applicants who do not share their religious beliefs, the ministries are likely to renounce the funds rather than comply. America's poor would initially suffer; later, taxpayers would, when they are forced to pay for services.

A second threat to the church is the proposal to eliminate a conscience clause that allows doctors, nurses, and pharmacists to refuse to provide "care" (that is, abortions) or drugs that violate their consciences. Killing the conscience clause would weaken Christians' role in providing health care and compromise health-care providers' First Amendment rights.

The White House also wants to reduce the charitable gift tax deduction for wealthy donors. The Tax Policy Center says this would have the unintended consequence of reducing charitable giving by $9 billion.

Why would anyone want to weaken the little platoons that run our churches, schools, charities, and think tanks, and that furnish services to the poor and suffering? Part of the answer: government bureaucrats have a voracious appetite for power—I know, I was one. They want to control vast sums of money.

We see the same trend toward government control in education. Congress is letting vouchers for 1,700 poor kids in the District of Columbia expire. These vouchers got kids out of some of America's worst public schools and into safe private ones. Why would Congress do this? Instead of vouchers, President Obama and most Democrats favor charter schools, which are government institutions—and thus acceptable to teachers' unions and bureaucrats.

Perhaps the most important intermediate structure—the family—will be irreparably damaged if our courts impose so-called same-sex marriage by judicial fiat, as in Iowa, Connecticut, and Massachusetts. As we noted earlier, in Scandinavian countries that recognized same-sex unions, heterosexual marriages immediately declined. With the exclusivity of marriage eliminated, couples evidently see little point in tying the knot—which means more children born out of wedlock. For thirty-three years I have witnessed in our prisons the consequences of family breakdown: a flood of dysfunctional and often dangerous kids.

Alexis de Tocqueville understood the vital role America's little platoons play. Voluntary associations, he argued, are a buffer against the all-powerful state, which has a natural tendency to want to take from individuals "the trouble of thinking and the pain of living," turning citizens into "timid and industrious animals, of which the government is the shepherd."

Hannah Arendt, a brilliant twentieth century political theorist, observed this phenomenon firsthand in Germany, describing in her classic book *The Origins of Totalitarianism* how totalitarian regimes succeed by the atomization of society—creating a mass of individuals isolated from the structures that hold civilized societies together. The result is that individuals are left to stand alone before the immense power of the state.

America is far from this, but when I realize how easily it could happen, I am reminded of the unknown man who, in 1989, bravely stood alone in Tiananmen Square before a row of Chinese army tanks. Ensuring this doesn't happen in the U.S. is a solemn responsibility of every Christian.

## It's Not about Power

The church can play a vital role in protecting the individual from the threat of totalitarianism. But increasingly, it seems that the involvement of conservative Christians in politics is not welcomed by the press or the wielders of political power. As each election approaches, politically minded conservative evangelicals are discovering they are not involved in the issues so much as they are the issue. "Religious Right Shows Its Muscle" read a headline in the *Chicago Tribune*. The *Arizona Republic* warned that "the religious right is causing near-civil war in some campaigns." The buzz on Capitol Hill today, as it has been in several recent elections, is that the Religious Right is splitting conservative ranks.

But this bellicose imagery could cause real harm to evangelical political activity.

Before the 2000 election, massive press attention was triggered when Jim Dobson gave his celebrated speech threatening to abandon the Republican Party. Worried party leaders convened a Values Summit and agreed to take action on such things as abortion and the marriage penalty.

Dobson did a noble service in jarring Congress out of its lethargy, but nothing sets off alarm bells in the press faster than political stirrings among the Religious Right. Journalists immediately warned in apocalyptic tones that religious conservatives were "marching on Washington" and "demanding their due."

Articles described Christians as a powerful voting bloc that delivered 45 percent of the vote in the 1994 Republican sweep of Congress. Many alluded to Ralph Reed's phrase that Christian conservatives are demanding "their place at the table" and depicted them in the same terms used for a labor union or any other special-interest group.

A decade after these criticisms were penned, the negative opinion of the press and the power mongers had not changed. Shortly after President Bush announced Samuel Alito's nomination, a senior U.S. senator sympathetic to Christian causes called me. "I know this will sound strange," he began, "but could you get some of your conservative religious friends to downplay their support for Judge Alito?" Their opposition to Harriet Miers, he explained, had actually aided her political prospects. But the day Alito was announced, a pro-life leader boasted, "We are now on the fast track to derailing *Roe v. Wade.*" This kind of talk could kill Alito's chances, the senator warned.

We're seen as doing more harm than good when backing judicial nominees, which tells us that media-driven stereotypes about the Religious Right have stuck. How often have you heard the press talk about the Religious Right wanting to "impose" its views on Americans, even comparing it to the Taliban? It's an outrageous charge, because no private group in a democracy can "impose" views. We Christians simply contend for our position in the open market.

Whether the stereotypes are fair or not, though, it's time to take some of the criticism to heart. I shudder every time I hear triumphalistic statements by Christian leaders, because they feed such fears—and understandably so, when a Christian leader predicts God's wrath on the people of Dover, Pennsylvania, for rejecting alternatives to evolution in their school curriculum. If we are honest, we must admit that we often act as if we're powerful because we have—or say we have—big constituencies. For example, after President Bush's 2004 reelection, Christian leaders argued they deserved payback for delivering the votes for his victory. Some even warned the president that if he didn't support a ban on so-called gay marriage, they wouldn't support his Social Security reforms.

These leaders may have been well-intentioned, but this was pure power brokering—the kind that allows our critics to say we're equating the Christian faith with a political agenda. We have to remember that we owe whatever influence we have to the moral authority we derive from serving God, not from the number of names on our mailing list.

To seek political victories in this heavy-handed way is not only a bad witness; it's also unwise. Ultimately, we need both political victories and cultural support. Even if President Bush's judicial appointees tip the Court into reversing *Roe v. Wade* (as I pray will happen), would there be fewer abortions? Not immediately. The issue would then return to the fifty states, and we'd have fifty battles instead of one. Of course, the law is a moral teacher, but changing the law is an empty victory unless we also change the moral consensus.

To change the culture, therefore, we must learn how to engage the political process more winsomely. It will require a different mindset. We'll need to recognize that we're appealing to hearts and minds, not twisting arms. In fact as well as in appearance, we are not seeking to impose, but rather to propose.

We're not demanding something for ourselves; we are inviting a hungry and needy world to come to Christ and find goodness and fullness of life. The Christian church makes a Great Proposal, inviting everyone to the table—regardless of ethnic origin, background, or economic status. We're inviting people to consider a worldview that's livable, that makes sense, in which people can discover *shalom* and human flourishing.

This means, first, loving those we contend against in the political process. Martin Luther King Jr. said, "Whom you would change, you must first love." Some Christian leaders do get this. The late Jerry Falwell, whatever else he did, went out of his way to engage the gay community protesting against him. Dobson set a similar example when protestors surrounded the Focus headquarters.

Second, we offer our strongest witness when we demonstrate that we do love others by fighting AIDS in Africa or the worldwide sex-trafficking trade, or by reforming prisons and prisoners, loving the most unlovable.

Our cultural mandate requires us to work for justice and righteousness so that God's creation reflects his majesty and goodness. That includes engaging in politics. But we must remember as we do this that we are proposing a more excellent way to a needy society, and that we do so in love, no matter how much abuse is heaped upon us.

## EARNING MORAL AUTHORITY

When the world sees us working for human rights, we earn moral authority that blunts the "imposing your morality" attacks in the public square. One *New York Times* columnist who vehemently opposes our political efforts has nonetheless praised Christians for the work he's seen us perform around the world.

Another reporter asked, "Why are evangelicals so concerned about AIDS in Africa and sex trafficking and slavery in Sudan? I thought all you cared about was abortion and gay rights." The reporter from a prestigious journal who had been following the Bush administration's foreign policy initiatives stumbled onto a curious fact: evangelicals were behind most of them.

The reporter's question gave me a wonderful opportunity to explain that evangelicals believe in the sanctity and dignity of *all* human life—not just unborn children, but also Sudanese slaves, sex trafficking victims, and Africans with AIDS.

The reporter got it; her subsequent front-page story contained unusual praise for evangelicals. This experience offers an insight on how we can make a powerful witness.

Over the past few years, evangelicals have actively promoted a morally grounded foreign policy. A decade ago, when no one was talking about the horror of sex trafficking, conservative activist Bill Bennett and I—prodded by the indefatigable human rights champion Michael Horowitz—helped organize a coalition to fight this evil. We testified to Congress in opposition to the Clinton administration, which had caved in to radical feminists who argued that prostitution should be redefined as "sex work"—just another empowering career option, like nursing or teaching.

Because of the leadership of Christians like Frank Wolf, Chris Smith, Joe Pitts, and others in Congress, legislation passed in 2000 authorizing sanctions. When the Bush administration took over, it appointed an "abolitionist"—gutsy former Congressman John Miller—to lead the trafficking office.

During his speech to the United Nations in 2003, President Bush powerfully decried the "special evil" of sex trafficking. The reporter interviewing me said she was astonished by the president's speech—raising moral issues before the U.N.? "Was this informed by his faith?" she asked.

Evangelicals led by Franklin Graham aroused our consciences over Africans with AIDS. The president himself was passionate, but he faced much opposition—particularly because he supported the ABC program (abstinence first, being monogamous, condoms only if necessary). Several of us met with the president and helped mobilize the Christian community. The result: a $15 billion package that not only treats the sick but also prevents AIDS through abstinence.

Then there's slavery in Sudan—the first matter Bennett and I raised with White House political strategist Karl Rove after President Bush was elected. The administration got tough, appointing former Senator John Danforth as special envoy, and the evangelical community flexed its muscles to move Congress. The result: the Sudan Peace Act, which has given us the best chance ever to end the slavery and genocide.

President Bush clearly had this moral agenda in mind. He made his first human-rights appeal in an eloquent but little-noted speech to the American Jewish Committee in May 2001. Then, in his Whitehall Palace speech in November 2003, he defended morally based foreign policy. The staid British audience was in awe as the president spoke of tracing our nation's spiritual roots to Britain's evangelical movement of the eighteenth and nineteenth centuries. He spoke of the "tireless compassion of Lord Shaftes-bury, the righteous courage of Wilberforce," and of the Good News "translated by Tyndale, preached by Wesley, lived out in the example of William Booth."

"The deepest beliefs of our nations set the direction of our foreign policy," the president said. "We value our own civil rights, so we stand for the human rights of others. We affirm the God-given dignity of every person, so we are moved to action by poverty and oppression and famine and disease."

So it must be with today's evangelicals. Following in the steps of Wilberforce, we must confront the moral horrors of our day. And when we work for causes that people across the political spectrum understand as promoting human good, we break out of the stereotypical "Bible-thumping bigot" mold.

We don't do it for that reason, of course; we do it because it is our calling. But when the world sees us defending the poor, the enslaved, the persecuted, and the sex trafficking victim, our arguments about protecting the unborn and the dignity of all human life have credibility.

This credibility extends all the way to the pages of the *New York Times*, where columnist Nicholas Kristof recently wrote: "I've lost my cynicism about evangelical groups partly because I've seen them at work abroad."

To much of the watching world, our determined concern for "the least of these" in every land may be our most powerful witness.

# 14

## THE KEY TO A UNIFIED SOCIETY

# 14

## THE KEY TO A
## UNIFIED SOCIETY

There's also an identity crisis bubbling just under the surface in the United States.[1] In his book, *Who Are We?*, scholar Samuel P. Huntington documents several challenges to a cohesive sense of American identity. First, while early settlers and immigrants were never ethnically homogenous, they largely traded in the same Anglo-Protestant cultural currency. But as twenty-first century demographic trends increasingly draw people from other quadrants of the world, shared cultural assumptions erode.

Exacerbating the problem is a rise in dual citizenship and more subnational identities, which have created divided loyalties. Meanwhile, in the business community, an increasingly globalized economy has caused leaders to adopt a more transnational identity, what some call "Davos man." And aside from a temporary resurgence of patriotism after September 11, Huntington documents how academic elites have led the way in devaluing patriotism and American history.

We rightly pride ourselves on our multiethnic, multiracial society. But as our society grows ever more diverse, how will we understand our national identity?

Huntington poses four possible solutions. The first is a creedal community whose identity exists only in a social contract embodied in the Declaration of Independence and other founding documents. This has historically provided cohesion. The next option is a bifurcated America, one that is bilingual and bicultural like Canada or Belgium. The third option is an exclusivist or imperial notion of America. And the last alternative, the one Huntington clearly favored, is a reinvigorated core culture and religion coupled with the earlier solution of a reinvigorated creedal community.

Can a Christian worldview inform us as we wrestle with our national identity? Any kind of racially or ethnically intolerant society would be incompatible with Christian principles. Further, we know that the core values of our creeds, which in particular promote the dignity of all people, resonate with Scripture and are worth preserving. American patriotism does not rest on jingoistic nationalism but on a universal creed that says, "All men are . . . endowed by their Creator with certain unalienable rights."

Liberty is one of those unalienable rights. And this core value, also emphasized in Scripture, teaches us that we cannot force beliefs on others. Our founders understood, however, that freedom of religion is not synonymous with expunging religion from public life, a problem that I and others addressed in the 2009 Manhattan Declaration. So if Huntington is in fact right that the U.S. needs a reinvigorated religious commitment, it won't come from a nation-mandated religion but rather from a re-invigorated populace.

## THE RISE OF SPIRITUAL ILLITERACY

One cause of America's identity crisis that may well stem from multiculturalism is the loss of a common understanding of certain deeply rooted principles and concepts. Only a few decades ago these concepts could be expressed in simple allusions or phrases drawn from a source for values and worldview that the country as a whole held in common. Two examples will demonstrate.

June 1940: Hitler's armies are poised to destroy the cornered British Army, stranded on the beaches at Dunkirk. As the British people anxiously await word of their fate, a three-word message is transmitted from the besieged army: "And if not."

The British public instantly recognizes the message—a reference to the words of Shadrach, Meshach, and Abednego standing before King Nebuchadnezzar's fiery furnace in Daniel 3. "Our God is able to save us . . . *and if not*, we will remain faithful to him anyway." The message galvanizes the British people. Thousands cross the English Channel in boats to rescue their army.

January 2001: America's newly elected president delivers his inaugural address. Commenting on it, Dick Meyer of CBS News confesses, "There were a few phrases in the speech I just didn't get. One was, 'When we see that wounded traveler on the road to Jericho, we will not pass to the other side.'" Meyer concludes, "I hope there's not a quiz."

What a difference six decades make. For centuries, biblical references were the common coinage of Western speech. As Dunkirk demonstrates, citizens were so steeped in the Scriptures that they immediately recognized a cryptic biblical allusion. But today that memory has been erased. Consider: pollster George Barna says only a small percentage of Americans can name the Ten Commandments, and only 42 percent can identify who preached the Sermon on the Mount. As Oxford theologian Alister McGrath explains, "In an increasingly secular culture, fewer and fewer people outside the Christian community have any real understanding of what Christians believe."

This spiritual illiteracy represents a sobering predicament for the church: how can we evangelize neighbors who no longer recognize, let alone think, in Christian terms—people to whom the language and literature of our faith is, for all intents and purposes, a foreign tongue?

We can begin by reintroducing our nation's children to the Bible in the public school classroom. Yes, it's legal—if we go about it the right way. Since the 1950s, many public-school kids have taken part in Released Time Bible Education, in which students leave campus during school hours to study Scripture devotionally. But the courts have also consistently upheld the academic study of the Bible *within* the classroom. Students can focus on the Bible as a literary text, learning the major narratives, symbols, and characters of the Bible. They can also learn how profoundly Biblical teachings have influenced Western drama, poetry, and fiction. After all, how can kids fully appreciate the works of Shakespeare, Milton, or classics like *Uncle Tom's Cabin* without some familiarity with the Scriptures?

Students may also study the Bible in history class, learning about the many historical documents that contain biblical references and how Americans invoke Scripture in debates ranging from abolition and temperance to civil rights and abortion—how, for instance, Martin Luther King Jr.'s "I Have A Dream" speech alludes in part to Isaiah. Can people be good citizens if they don't know their own history?

Teaching about the Bible in this manner will not be easy: the ACLU and other naysayers will be lurking in school hallways, ready to sue any district that steps out of line. To help schools navigate the legal minefields, the Bible Literacy Project has developed a Bible curriculum for use in public schools that will pass constitutional muster. To ensure balance, a coalition ranging from the American Jewish Committee to the National Association of Evangelicals to the American Federation of Teachers reviewed it. And to encourage school boards, the crack lawyers of the Becket Fund have offered to defend, gratis, any school district that is sued.

The Bible Literacy Project tells parents how to introduce the curriculum into their schools, and answers concerns that parents of all faiths might have about it. Some critics fear that merely studying the Bible's role in history, or as literature, diminishes it. I disagree. Educating the culture in this way is what Francis Schaeffer called pre-evangelism. Christians can then take the next step, explaining why the Scriptures have had this effect; that indeed it is the Word of God that moves citizens to action. The stakes are high. Values are transmitted from one generation to the next by what sociologist Robert Bellah calls the "community of memory."

We must decide if we want our language seasoned with biblical references or with vulgar and often uncharitable idioms. It would be a spiritual dereliction not to grasp the opportunity to reinstate Christianity as our cultural currency.

## Learning the Language of Culture

The loss of biblical literacy has created a unique challenge to Christians who want to affect the culture with the Christian worldview. When the culture no longer understands our language, we must learn to speak in terms they understand. If the culture has lost its memory of our language, we must learn theirs. The following incident illustrates why this is imperative.

Thirteen-year-old Tim scanned his weekly quiz in Earth Science and read: "Where did the earth come from?" Without thinking, he scribbled: "God created it." The next day, his test came back with a big red check mark and 20 points chopped off his grade. The expected answer was the Big Bang.

When Tim's mother told the members of her Bible-study group, where my wife, Patty, attends, they were indignant. Go show that teacher what the Bible says, they urged. It's right there in Genesis: *God* created the heaven and the earth.

But when I heard the story, I startled Tim's mother by calling her up: don't charge into class, Bible in hand, I warned. To the teacher, that's religion; his class is on science. Instead, ask him scientific questions: How did the Big Bang itself get started? Something can't come out of nothing, so what caused the Big Bang?

For centuries, conventional scientific wisdom taught that the universe was eternal. But Big Bang theory has given dramatic evidence that the universe had a beginning—just as Scripture teaches. And if the Big Bang is the origin of the universe, its cause must be something beyond the universe, a transcendent cause.

These exciting philosophical questions are being debated by astronomers today. So why shouldn't students learn them, too? Christians ought to argue for more academic freedom, not less. We should challenge *bad* science with *better* science.

Whenever I make this point publicly, I can count on a deluge of letters from Christians asking, "What's wrong with quoting the Bible?" A radio station once threatened to take my radio program *BreakPoint* off the air. "It's heresy to tell believers not to cite their Bibles," the station manager fumed.

But this reaction reflects a confusion widespread among Christians between saving grace and common grace. In preaching and evangelism, we are instruments of God's saving grace— and we preach his Word boldly, confident that it never returns empty. God's Word cuts to the heart like a two-edged sword.

But in the bulk of our lives, we are instruments of God's *common* grace or providence—his work of maintaining creation by promoting righteousness and restraining evil. As his servants in this task, we are in the world (though not of it), and we should translate God's truth into the language of the world: speaking to scientists in the language of science, to artists in the language of art, to politicians in the language of politics.

Since the Fall, the world has been subject to evil and corruption, but it is still under God's dominion. And believers are still called, as Genesis 1 says, to be God's vice-regents, exercising his dominion in every area of life. Theologians call this the cultural mandate: we express the image of God by searching out the underlying structure of creation and shaping and forming it—by inventing things and developing civilizations.

In our vocation and our social circles, we are to work to build up the society where God has placed us, arguing persuasively for the principles that make for good families, good businesses, good political structures—and yes, good science education.

These basic principles are accessible to nonbelievers as well as believers, because they too are created in the image of God and live in God's creation. Our task is to communicate the truths of Scripture by translating them into contemporary language. As the late Francis Schaeffer taught, we need to treat modern culture as a mission field, working as hard as any foreign missionary at translating our message into language our listeners understand. For even if they speak English, they think in different conceptual categories, which we must learn and master in order to communicate effectively.

For example, at Prison Fellowship we contend for biblical principles of justice using prudential arguments in the public square. I've spoken to many state legislatures and before congressional committees, arguing that it makes no sense to let non-dangerous prison inmates remain idle behind bars. Why not require them to work, earning money to pay restitution to their victims?

Once someone sees the merit of an idea, that may become an opportunity for witness. Whenever I discuss restitution, invariably some politician will say, "Great idea. Where did it come from?" And I'll reply, "Do you have a Bible at home? Dust it off and look up Exodus. What I'm recommending is exactly what God told Moses thousands of years ago on Mount Sinai." Effective principles of criminal justice are rooted squarely in scriptural truth.

When your children come home from school with big red checks marked on their tests, don't rush into the classroom brandishing your Bible. Instead, let's find ways to translate biblical truth into prudential principles that nonbelievers understand and find persuasive. This work may not save souls, but it is the way we obey God's command to promote righteousness and hold back the forces of evil in society. It is a means of common grace.

There is no substitute for God's Word in the saving work of leading the world to Christ. And there is no substitute for scripturally based prudential arguments in the preserving work of restraining evil and building civilization.

## RECALLING THE NATION TO ITS HERITAGE

I am not suggesting that we force the nation's citizens to learn the Bible. I am simply saying that its principles are ingrained in our national heritage and founding principles, and we ignore its influence on America to our own peril. Whether Christian, Jew, Muslim, Hindu, or atheist, we cannot preserve our liberties unless we recognize and understand the biblically drawn principles that form the foundation of our democracy.

I believe that for national identity to be salient in the midst of our changing society, we need to promote a recommitment to our creeds, a respect for American history, and a proper role of patriotism, rooted in love of neighbor. Our founders' Judeo-Christian heritage helped produce a culture in which moral responsibility, transcendent ethical principles, and the dignity of all people could flourish—a culture in which our creedal values made sense. This is why our role as leaven within society is so important, and why we must continue to bring a biblical influence to the public square, reinvigorating society.

As we do so, we must guard against the easy tendency to embrace xenophobic notions or fall into the equally perilous trap of promoting subcultural identities over national identity. People will not live with, let alone die for, a nation that has abandoned its religious moorings and adopted a creed that suggests we simply live together in cosmopolitan bliss. Millions of us, however, have been willing to live and die for beliefs rooted in our deepest convictions about God and man—convictions that were expressed so well in the stirring words of our national creed, the Declaration of Independence.

# 15

## BEING THE CHURCH WHEREVER YOU ARE

# 15

## BEING THE CHURCH
## WHEREVER YOU ARE

For those who think the Reformation no longer influences American life, I recommend a trip to western Michigan.[1] I was there a few years ago for the dedication of the Rich and Helen DeVos Arts and Worship Center at Grand Rapids Christian High School. Everything about it was impressive, designed with excellence. Rich DeVos, who was born in Grand Rapids and attended that school, has never lost his love for his community, which he expresses through his philanthropy.

DeVos is not alone. Driving through western Michigan neighborhoods, you see on building after building the names of Dutch Reformed families who settled that area: the Van Andel Medical Institute, the DeVos Children's Hospital, the Prince Conference Center at Calvin College, the DeWitt, DePree, and Cook buildings at Hope College. And names like Huizenga, Volkema, and Jansma fill the corporate offices that are widely respected for community endeavors.

Devotion like this reflects a Christian commitment to

community, in sharp contrast to what's happening elsewhere in our culture. This era will be remembered for the business scandals in which corporate raiders cooked books, bilked stockholders, left employees in the lurch, and then fled to mansions on faraway beaches.

What makes western Michigan citizens so different is their heritage. A hardy and industrious people, the Dutch arrived in Michigan and Iowa in the mid-nineteenth century explicitly to plant, as historian John Bratt put it, "Christian communities to serve as radiating centers of the gospel." They reflected "cultural Calvinism," which reached its zenith in nineteenth-century Holland. It emphasized the lordship of Christ and sphere sovereignty—the belief that each institution in society has its ordained role.

This Reformation-influenced vision continues, which is why Ottawa County was so successful when, a few years ago, then-Governor John Engler challenged Michigan counties to get jobs for all able-bodied welfare recipients. Ottawa County asked its 250 churches to help; sixty signed up. Within a year, the welfare rolls were emptied.

This commitment to community is why the descendants of the original settlers have continued to plow their profits back into their hometowns—residents like the late Edgar Prince and his family, who led efforts to gut downtown Holland (seat of Ottawa County) and totally rebuild it. The family even started a restaurant knowing it would lose money. Why? Because it serves as the local gathering place, fostering a sense of community—like the coffee shops of an earlier era. The town's benefactors self-consciously worked at giving citizens a sense of attachment, and then passed their values on to succeeding generations.

Christians should emulate this caring about community, especially the soil in which they were reared. Remember, the faith began as communities of believers living in a hostile culture. The particulars of time and place help shape our identity.

One great scholar, Russell Kirk, not only wrote about the importance of roots and tradition, but also lived it. Not long before he died in 1994, I visited Kirk at his home in Mecosta, Michigan. Now, Mecosta isn't much more than a truck stop in the boonies. But Kirk stayed put, inconvenient though it was, because six generations of his family had lived there. A true conservative, he had a keen sense of place and belonging.

In today's mobile culture, not everybody can stay in their hometowns, as Kirk did, or as so many Dutch immigrants have. Social and economic factors—the post-World War II economic explosion, easy air travel, and sprawling international companies—have eroded our sense of connection to communities. But we can sink our roots into the towns we now call home. The principle remains: what we produce in and from our communities we should return to them.

Most of America used to be like Ottawa County. Civic duty was once a cardinal American virtue, so much so that Tocqueville commented that there weren't ten men in all of France who did what Americans did every day as a matter of course—raising barns, feeding the hungry, and looking after orphans. Christians must set the example for recovering this tradition and rejuvenating in our communities the sense of responsibility the Dutch Reformed citizens of western Michigan demonstrate.

C. S. Lewis, who lived in the same Oxford house most of his adult life, put it well: as Christians, we can't love the whole world. But we should remember that God has placed us in a specific community at a particular time. We're called to love those around us. Loving them means serving them—and in doing so, we become the best of citizens.

## INDIVIDUALS WHO MADE A DIFFERENCE

What I saw in western Michigan is a microcosm of what it means to be the church. The church is a body, a community of individuals, each committed to the values, mission, and worldview of the whole and displaying those commitments in his or her individual sphere of influence. When individuals, each acting in his or her own sphere of activity, display the values and characteristics of the church community, the culture of the nation will be ultimately affected and changed.

The driving force in American life are those previously mentioned "habits of the heart," as Tocqueville called them—the individual dispositions and tastes that shape the country's moral consensus. So regardless of who occupies the Oval Office, the culture war will be waged in the neighborhoods where people live. And if we are prepared, we can succeed on this battleground.

Take the example of Lisa Hunter from a liberal community in the Southwest. While tidying her kitchen one Saturday, she came across her twelve-year-old daughter Ashley's science test. Ashley had checked "primeval explosion" for a question on the universe's origin.

Lisa sat Ashley down and gently asked, "Did you really believe what you wrote?" Ashley burst into tears. "No," she said, "but that was the answer the teacher wanted."

Lisa raised the issue at a parent-teacher conference, but when she began discussing evidence for intelligent design the teacher cut her off. "I'm not allowed to teach about religion," she said dismissively.

But Lisa had done her homework. Having read books on Darwin and intelligent design, she had learned how to argue from a scientific standpoint against naturalistic philosophy. Lisa headed for the principal's office and made her case. The principal startled Lisa by acknowledging that her arguments made sense. She then instructed Ashley's teacher to apologize to her students and explain that there are conflicting theories about evolution.

Then a further surprise: the principal was so impressed with Lisa's knowledge that she invited her to serve on the school's curriculum committee.

At a time when Christians are losing political fights over evolution—famously as a decade ago in Kansas, where conservative school-board members were vilified and defeated at the polls—we can still make our case one-on-one. Surprising numbers of our neighbors and even teachers are on our side: according to Gallup, 68 percent favor the teaching of evolution and creation.

We can influence other cultural arenas as well. Government, for example, can do little to censor smut, but Christians as private citizens can get results. Take the case of Abercrombie & Fitch, the onetime outfitter of country gentlemen, now among the hippest clothing stores for teens. One Abercrombie catalog featured nudity, alcoholic recipes, and explicit sex advice. In response, parents' groups organized protests at stores and MADD (Mothers Against Drunk Driving) unleashed its heavy artillery. The company backed down and recalled the offensive catalog. More tellingly, Abercrombie subsequently reported a sharp decline in sales. The *Wall Street Journal* attributed it to teen fickleness. I wonder.

These are small victories but not isolated examples. Christians across the country are learning how to present their case effectively. A decade ago, teenage pregnancies dropped to a sixty-year low. Government officials attributed the drop to sex-education programs. The real reason, I believe, was the multitude of church-based programs like True Love Waits along with shifting public attitudes. Habits of the heart provide restraints government can't begin to impose.

Another example: the courts may, as they did in 2000, forbid us from witnessing to pregnant women as they enter abortion clinics. But we can reduce abortion by volunteering at crisis pregnancy centers—performing sonograms, telling pregnant teens about adoption, and taking homeless moms into our homes.

We may not be able to close the floodgates of Hollywood pollution, but youth leaders can invite teens over to watch good films, explaining how the filmmaker's worldview compares to biblical teachings. Or we can join the growing numbers of faith-based ministries that tutor inner-city children, help teens get off drugs, or take needy kids to Christian camps.

In 1994, conservative leader Bill Bennett stunned a crowd of Christian activists mobilizing for the fall election. "Politics matters," he told them, "but the solution to what ails us . . . lies beyond politics. It lies with a change of the heart." Bennett urged the group, "Stay involved in politics if you wish," but also work to change culture.

Wise counsel. Regardless of any election's outcome, or the triumphalistic promises or dire rhetoric you may hear, each of us should remain steady at our post in the nearest theater of war: our neighborhood.

## The Congressman Who Made a Difference

For most of us, being the church in the world means being involved in our communities and neighborhoods. But in the larger scope of things, your "neighborhood" is wherever you are. Being the church simply means living the image of Christ in whatever field you're placed—even if that field is politics, as it is for Congressman Frank Wolf.

Frank Wolf (R-Va.) is not much at glad-handing, and he shies away from the limelight. For his serene optimism, critics have labeled him naive. His travels are not the typical junkets to posh resorts or embassy parties but risky excursions to outposts ravaged by war and famine—especially to places where fellow Christians are persecuted for their faith.

His most recent journey took him to Tibet, where he posed as a tourist, eluded the tour guide by pretending to be ill, and then sneaked out to talk to Tibetans on the street for the real story of Chinese repression. Another expedition took him to Sudan, a nation waging a self-described religious war against its own citizens who are Christians or other non-Muslims through a campaign of torture, starvation, and murder. Sudanese soldiers are literally snatching children from their mothers' arms and selling them into slavery for the price of a few head of cattle. Girls are sold as concubines.

Wolf has journeyed to East Timor to report on massacres conducted by the Indonesian government. He has dodged bombs in Nagorno Karabakh. He has investigated conditions in El Salvador, Bosnia, and Ethiopia. Instead of enjoying the plush accommodations he could command as a government official, Wolf toughs it out with ordinary people for a first-hand sense of their plight.

Before the fall of the Iron Curtain, Wolf tramped throughout Eastern Europe championing for freedom. He was the first American official to bulldog his way into the notorious Perm Camp 35 in the Siberian gulag, where leading dissidents were imprisoned. Upon returning, he publicized the religious and political abuses they reported and arranged for me to join a second group visiting the camp. Due to Wolf's tenacity, the Soviets released many prisoners even before the USSR collapsed.

What makes this unusual politician so different? The secret is his Christian faith. His inspiration is the same nineteenth-century British politician and passionate evangelical we've mentioned numerous times in this book, William Wilberforce.

For his indefatigable efforts, Wolf has won grudging respect even from people on the opposite side of his conservative politics. Liberal columnist Mary McGrory calls him "a watchman on the rampart of world freedom." The late Democratic congressman Lionel Van Deerlin described Wolf as one of "a special breed," who "seem attracted to public office to fulfill more than personal or political ends." Men like Wolf, he added, "sustain a flicker of hope in the elective process."

In 1998, Wolf, with Senate co-sponsor Sen. Arlen Specter, introduced the Freedom from Religious Persecution Act, which would impose sanctions on nations that persecute people for their religious faith—places like Sudan, Egypt, Iran, Saudi Arabia, Vietnam, and China. The act started out as a motherhood measure: who could possibly be against protecting people from religious persecution? The bill quickly won widespread support, and congressional leaders promised to bring it to a vote.

Shortly afterward, the bill encountered fierce opposition from lobbyists because the sanctions it imposed against violators would cause economic losses to a few American companies. But Wolf stuck by his guns and refused to give up, and the bill was finally passed over the opposition.

## Why Do Christians Do It?

Throughout the history of our nation Christians have been at the forefront of reform, resistance to tyranny, and infringement on freedom. Why do Christians do these things when they could more easily turn their heads the other way and simply live their lives in quiet safety, hunkering down beneath the radar?

*Contra mundum* first came to my attention while reading a letter penned by John Wesley to that indefatigable public servant and abolitionist, William Wilberforce. In it, Wesley compared Wilberforce to Athanasius, an earlier champion of Christ's cause who had stood "against the world," defending the Nicene doctrine of the Trinity against Arian heretics. My friend Richard John Neuhaus would later pick up the phrase and add another—"against the world for the world"—to describe the modern-day reform movement, eventually known as the Hartford Appeal. Neuhaus, Wesley, Wilberforce, and Athanasius all knew that true love for one's neighbor sometimes means standing against the world for the world's sake.

While recently reading Peter Kreeft's wonderful book, *The God Who Loves You*, I was reminded that almost every prominent modern-day apologist has written at least one book about love. Alongside their tomes defending the tenets of the faith, C. S. Lewis, Francis Schaeffer, Norman Geisler, Ravi Zacharias, Art Lindsley, and Kreeft have all turned their attention to studying the many facets of love. Why did each of them take time from their urgent calling to write a book on what some might consider a strange subject for apologists?

While these apologists took the stance of being *against* the world—against the false worldviews of their day—they took that stance because they were *for* the world, wanting the world's ultimate good. Love is the true apologist's motive, the *animus*. It is also the *telos*, or end goal: Since God is love, understanding the true nature of love means helping people understand the true nature of God. And if these weren't reasons enough, these writers have learned that love itself is the greatest apologetic.

Yet so many have misunderstood love's meaning because the English language has only one word to describe its many emotions and objects. The Greek writers were more nuanced. Love can be *eros*, the romantic kind that we celebrate each February, or *storge*, meaning affinity and affection, or *phileo*, brotherly fondness, or finally *agape*, God's self-denying love. The first three refer to emotions, but agape is an objective state. It is true love. One of the main arguments for atheism, Kreeft warns, stems from a confusion between objective love and mere emotions such as kindness. After all, how could a good God permit suffering in the world?

"*Agape* wills the objective good of the beloved," writes Kreeft. "Thus it wills or tolerates suffering when suffering is necessary for the beloved's true, objective good." He goes on to explain that this is why loving parents discipline their children, and why God does not wipe every tear away until his return. While *agape* often overlaps with kindness and is always teeming with emotion, God still takes a long-range view of the beloved's best interest. God's pure self-forgetful gift-love has a perfect view of the beloved's needs and true fulfillment.

If knowing God is the greatest objective good for humans, then the aim of real love is helping others know God. It means displacing false gods from the throne of the one true God. It means helping the beloved find that which truly satisfies. Lewis writes in *The Four Loves* that the lesser loves begin to become demons the moment they begin to become gods. That is why Christ tells us, "If any man come to me, and hate not his father, and mother, and wife . . . and his own life also, he cannot be my disciple" (Luke 14:26 KJV).

Like Athanasius and Wilberforce—and like God himself—true love must sometimes take a stance of opposition for the objective good of the beloved. True love will dismantle false worldviews. True love will reveal where lesser loves have become gods. True love will be against the world for the world, because true love knows what the world needs most.

# NOTES

Every reasonable attempt has been made to locate the sources quoted in the original articles that appeared in *Christianity Today*. However, if there is any inadvertent omission or error, please contact the publisher so the proper adjustments can be made in future printings of this book.

INTRODUCTION

1. Material for this introduction is drawn from Charles Colson, "The Sky Isn't Falling," *Christianity Today*, January 11, 1999.

CHAPTER 1

1. This chapter is drawn from the following columns first published in *Christianity Today:* "The New Civil War," January 19, 2005; "The Sky Isn't Falling," January 11, 1999; "Worldview Boot Camp," December 1, 2004; "The Postmodern Crackup," December 1, 2003; "How Evil Became Cool," August 9, 1999; and "Channeling Populist Rage," April 6, 2010.

CHAPTER 2

1. This chapter is drawn from the following columns first published in *Christianity Today:* "Poster Boy for Postmodernism," November 16, 1998; "The Devil in the DNA," August 10, 1998; "Madison Avenue's Spiritual Chic," January 12, 1998; and "More Doctrine, Not Less," April 22, 2002.

2. C. S. Lewis, *The Abolition of Man* (New York: HarperCollins, 1944, 1947, 1974), p. 26.

3. "Poll: Abortion Support Falling Among Young Adults," from *The Christian Post* website: http://www.christianpost.com/news/poll-abortion-support-falling-among-young-adults-44267/. Accessed February 17, 2011.

CHAPTER 3

1. This chapter is drawn from the following columns first published in *Christianity Today:* "Moral Education after Monica," March 1, 1999; "The Wages of Secularism," June 10, 2002; "Machiavellian Morality," September 22, 2005; "How the Courts Censor Morality," November 17, 1997; "The Moral Home Front," October 1, 2004; and "Checks and (Out of) Balance," March 5, 2001.

CHAPTER 4

1. This chapter is drawn from the following columns first published in *Christianity Today:* "Sowing Confusion," October 1, 2003; "Societal Suicide," June 1, 2004; "Why Not Gay Marriage?" October 28, 1996; and "Why Fidelity Matters," April 27, 1998.

CHAPTER 5

1. This chapter is drawn from the following columns first published in *Christianity Today:* "Jeremiah at Harvard," August 5, 2008; "Slouching into Sloth," April 23, 2001; "Violence in Media," June 11, 2001; "Cleanliness Is Next to Crimelessness," January 6, 1997; and "Violence in Media," June 11, 2001.

2. Aleksandr I. Solzhenitsyn, *A World Split Apart* (New York: Harper & Row, 1978).

3. News Release, The Henry J. Kaiser Family Foundation, November 9, 2005. http://www.kff.org/entmedia/entmedia110905nr.cfm. Accessed February 18, 2010.

4. "Teen Market to Surpass $200 Billion by 2011," Marketing Charts website, June 28, 2007. http://www.marketingcharts.com/interactive/teen-market-to-surpass-200-billion-by-2011-despite-population-decline-817/. Accessed February 18, 2011.

CHAPTER 6

1. This chapter is drawn from the following columns first published in *Christianity Today*: "Verdict that Demands Evidence," March 28, 2005; "Post-Truth Society," March 11, 2002; "A Serious Decay," December 31, 2008; "The Oxford Prophet," June 15, 1998; "Emerging Confusion," June 1, 2006; "Salad Bar Christianity," August 7, 2000; and "Community of Memory," October 15, 2007.

2. C. S. Lewis, "Answers to Questions on Christianity" in *God in the Dock* (Grand Rapids: Wm. B. Eerdmans, 1970), p. 52.

3. C. S. Lewis, *The Abolition of Man* (New York: HarperCollins, 1947), p. 60.

4. Ibid, p. 75.

5. C. S. Lewis, "The Poison of Subjectivism" in *Christian Reflections* (Grand Rapids: Wm. B. Eerdmans, 1967), p. 81.

6. "Barna Survey Examines Changes in Worldview Among Christians Over the Past 13 Years." Posted on the Barna Group website March 6, 2009. http://www.barna.org/transformation-articles/252-barna-survey-examines-changes-in-worldview-among-christians-over-the-past-13-years. Accessed February 19, 2011.

CHAPTER 7

1. This chapter is drawn from the following columns first published in *Christianity Today:* "Faith Vs. Statistics," February 1, 2003; "War on the Weak," December 4, 2006; "Undaunted," August 5, 2002; and "The New Tyranny," October 1, 2001.

2. C. S. Lewis, *The Abolition of Man* (New York: HarperCollins, 1944, 1947), p. 57.

3. Ibid., p. 58

4. Ibid., p. 72.

CHAPTER 8

1. This chapter is drawn from the following columns first published in *Christianity Today:* "Who Holds These Truths?" October 6, 1997; "Scout's Dishonor," November 15, 1999; "Bad Judgment," August 1, 2006; "The Earmark Epidemic," September 25, 2006; "The Political Message of Evangelicals," October 5, 1998; and "Voting Like It Matters," October 10, 2008.

2. http://en.wikipedia.org/wiki/Boy_Scouts_of_America_v._Dale#cite_ref-17.

3. From the BSA Counsel website: http://www.bsalegal.org/bsa-v.-wyman-207.asp

CHAPTER 9

1. This chapter is drawn from the following columns first published in *Christianity Today:* "A Serious Decay," December 31, 2008; "Pander Politics," January 8, 2001; "The Earmark Epidemic," September 25, 1998; "The Political Message of Evangelicals," October 5, 1998; and "Voting Like It Matters," October 10, 2008.

2. http://www.rasmussenreports.com/public_content/politics/mood_of_america/congressional_performance

3. http://membership.cagw.org/site/PageServer?pagename=reports_pig
   -book2005

CHAPTER 10

1. This chapter is drawn from the following columns first published in *Christianity Today:* "A Clan of One's Own," October 7, 2002; "The Lost Art of Commitment," August 4, 2010; "Why Women Like Big Government," November 11, 1996; "What Are We Doing Here?" December 5, 2003.

CHAPTER 11

1. This chapter is drawn from the following columns first published in *Christianity Today:* "Evangelical Drift," April 1, 2004; "Soothing Ourselves to Death," April 1, 2006; "Doctrine Bears Repeating," March 24, 2009; "Worldview Boot Camp," December 1, 2004; "Reclaiming Occupied Territory," August 1, 2004.

CHAPTER 12

1. This chapter is drawn from the following columns first published in *Christianity Today:* "Wake-Up Call," November 12, 2001; "The Moral Home Front," October 1, 2004; "Why We Should Be Hopeful," April 26, 1999; "The Invasion of God," December 6, 2007; and "A Healthy Cult," June 12, 2000.

CHAPTER 13

1. This chapter is drawn from the following columns first published in *Christianity Today:* "Protecting Our Little Platoons," June 10, 2009; "Promises, Promises," August 7, 2007; "A More Excellent Way," February 1, 2006; "Confronting Moral Horror," February 1, 2004.

CHAPTER 14

1. This chapter is drawn from the following columns first published in *Christianity Today:* "Who Are Americans?" June 21, 2010; "Reversing Biblical Memory Loss," August 6, 2001; and "Quoting the Bible Isn't Enough," August 11, 1997.

CHAPTER 15

1. This chapter is drawn from the following columns first published in *Christianity Today:* "Being Here," August 1, 2003; "Neighborhood Outpost," November 13, 2000; "Do We Love Coke More than Justice?" March 2, 1998; and "Valentine's Dynamic Love," February 12, 2010.

# Select Bibliography

Arendt, Hannah. *The Origins of Totalitarianism*. Garsington, UK: Benediction Books, 2009.

Budziszewski, J. *What We Can't Not Know: A Guide*. Spence, 2003; rev Ignatius Press, 2011.

The Commission on Children at Risk. *Hardwired to Connect: The New Scientific Case for Authoritative Communities*. New York: Broadway Publications, 2003.

Ellul, Jacques. *The Political Illusion*. New York: Vintage Books, 1972.

George, Robert P. *The Clash of Orthodoxies: Law, Religion and Morality in Crisis*. Wilmington, DE: Intercollegiate Studies Institute, 2002.

Kreeft, Peter. *The God Who Loves You: Love Divine, All Loves Excelling*. San Francisco: Ignatius Press, 2004.

Lewis, C. S. *The Abolition of Man*. New York: HarperCollins, 1944, 1947, 1974.

Popenoe, David. *Life without Father: Compelling New Evidence That Fatherhood and Marriage Are Indispensable for the Good of Children and Society*. Cambridge, MA: Harvard University Press, 1999.

Roof, Wade Clark, *Spiritual Marketplace: Baby Boomers and the Remaking of American Religion*. Princeton NJ: Princeton University Press, 1999.

**Charles Colson** is a popular and widely known author, speaker and radio commentator whose critiques of American culture have made him one of the nation's most prominent proponents of a biblical worldview. He is the founder of the international ministry Prison Fellowship and the Colson Center for Christian Worldview. Many of his books, such as *Born Again, The Body, Loving God, The Good Life, How Now Shall We Live?* and *The Faith,* have shaped modern Christian thinking on cultural issues and public policy.

In 1993 Colson was awarded the prestigious Templeton Prize for Progress in Religion, donating the entire $1 million prize to Prison Fellowship. And in 2008, Colson was honored by President Bush with the Presidential Citizen's Medal. His radio broadcast, *BreakPoint*, airs daily to 2 million listeners.